PENGUIN BOOKS

IT WAS A DARK AND STORMY NIGHT—
THE FINAL CONFLICT

✝ ✝ ✝ ✝ ✝ ✝ ✝

Scott Rice is a professor of English at San Jose State University and the creator of the Bulwer-Lytton Fiction Contest. Born in Lewiston, Idaho, and raised in Spokane, Washington, he received his B.A. from Gonzaga University and his M.A. and Ph.D. from the University of Arizona. Scott Rice is married and the father of three children: Jeremy, Matthew, and Elizabeth. He is also the compiler of *It Was a Dark and Stormy Night, Son of "It Was a Dark and Stormy Night,"* and *Bride of Dark and Stormy* (all available from Penguin).

EDWARD BULWER-LYTTON

IT WAS A DARK AND STORMY NIGHT: THE FINAL CONFLICT

Yet More of the Best (?) from the Bulwer-Lytton Fiction Contest

Compiled by
SCOTT RICE

Penguin Books

PENGUIN BOOKS
Published by the Penguin Group
Viking Penguin, a division of Penguin Books USA Inc.,
375 Hudson Street, New York, New York 10014, U.S.A.
Penguin Books Ltd, 27 Wrights Lane,
London W8 5TZ, England
Penguin Books Australia Ltd, Ringwood,
Victoria, Australia
Penguin Books Canada Ltd, 10 Alcorn Avenue, Suite 300,
Toronto, Ontario, Canada M4V 3B2
Penguin Books (N.Z.) Ltd, 182–190 Wairau Road,
Auckland 10, New Zealand

Penguin Books Ltd, Registered Offices:
Harmondsworth, Middlesex, England

First published in Penguin Books 1992

3 5 7 9 10 8 6 4 2

LIBRARY OF CONGRESS CATALOGING IN PUBLICATION DATA
It was a dark and stormy night: the final conflict: yet more of the
best (?) from the Bulwer-Lytton Fiction Contest/ compiled by Scott
Rice.
p.   cm.
ISBN 0 14 01.5791 3
1. Authorship—Humor. 2. Style, Literary—Humor. 3. Fiction—
Technique—Humor. 4. English language—Style—Humor. I. Rice,
Scott. II. Title: Bulwer-Lytton Fiction Contest.
PN6231.A77I8 1992
818'.540208—dc20   91-2501

Printed in the United States of America

Set in Caslon 540
Designed by Beth Tondreau Design

CONTENTS

INTRODUCTION vii

LYTTONY I 1

LIKE AN OVERRIPE BEEFSTEAK TOMATO 6

VILE PUNS 13

LAST NIGHT I DREAMT I WENT TO MANDERLY AGAIN 19

LYTTONY II 26

THE WAY WE LIVE NOW 31

A GUN IS NOTHING BUT A TWO-EDGED SWORD 38

MIKE HARDWARE, P.I. 43

LYTTONY III 50

PLAIN BROWN WRAPPERS 55

OLD DR. CRICKETT CALLED FOR NURSE JUNEBUG 62

THE FIRST DAY OF THE IDITAROD 68

LYTTONY IV 75

IN DUBIOUS TASTE 80

"E.T., GO HOME!" 85

LYTTONY V 91

THE WAY WE LOVE NOW 96

MORE VILE PUNS 102

"RUMBLING, SCHMUMBLING!" RETORTED BULONIUS 108

A DARK AND STORMY NIGHT 113

LYTTONY VI 118

INTRODUCTION

The Bulwer-Lytton Fiction Contest is an annual competition sponsored by San Jose State University that challenges entrants to compose the opening sentence to the worst of all possible novels. The contest takes its name from Edward George Bulwer-Lytton, an industrious Victorian novelist whose *Paul Clifford* (1830) set a standard for pot-boiling openers: "It was a dark and stormy night . . ." The following is the fourth collection of entries published by Penguin Books.

The Return of Bulwer-Lytton

Let us imagine for a few moments that Bulwer-Lytton himself has returned, stung back into life by a hundred and fifty years' worth of barbs hurled at his literary reputation, and all because he started one little sentence with "It was a dark and stormy night."

Okay, maybe the sentence was not so little. The unabridged original went on for fifty-one more words, an exercise in melodrama and prodigal verbosity:

It was a dark and stormy night; the rain fell in torrents—except at occasional intervals, when it was checked by a violent gust of wind which swept up the streets (for it is in London that our scene lies), rattling along the housetops, and fiercely agitating the scanty flame of the lamps that struggled against the darkness.   —*Paul Clifford*

Almost everybody has had fun with this one, even that cartoon beagle with the literary pretensions (Does anyone know why Charles Schulz hasn't gotten Snoopy a word processor yet and a subscription to *Writer's Digest*?).

Even the callowest applicants to the Famous Writers School could tidy up Bulwer's classic. For starters, what about "swept up the *London* streets," eliminating that clumsy parenthesis? And must we first say that there was a rain and then tell that it was falling in torrents? Couldn't we say that "the downpour was checked only by gusts of wind"? (But what other kinds of gusts are there?) That communicates the same idea, but in nine instead of nineteen words. But enough. We have to make antiquarian allowances sometimes. After all, literary tastes have changed. Modern readers like to be told less and shown more. Post-Hemingway readers even expect to figure out some things for themselves. Besides, Papa's version might have seemed just as unlikely to Bulwer's Victorian contemporaries:

> After dark a storm came and sometimes in the wind there was a noise on the rooftops, and you could see that the streetlamps were having a bad time.

Or something like that.

But let's say that Bulwer is back and prowling a local book vendor's, on a mission to see if his late-twentieth-century detractors have learned to open a novel any better. He has materialized in a typical American chain bookstore, one of those places where computers do all the ordering based on publishers' hype and market surveys, and where many of the bestsellers are ghostwritten for fallen politicians and Hollywood celebrities. Ghostwritten! Bulwer has the perfect resumé: a long list of credits, stuff turned into movies (*The Last Days of Pompeii*—three times!), and he's a real ghost.

Bulwer looks a little agog at the bright, bas-relief covers with their depictions of splendidly torsoed heroes and heroines. He scans the extravagant blurbs. Nothing there to make Victorian tastes seem lurid or heavy-handed by comparison, although in his day the engravings were all on the inside. But he feels a little naughty because all the overflowing bosoms put him in mind of Vesuvius.

It doesn't take him long to find a best-seller. Half the books in the store sport the label. He picks up *Love and Dreams*, by Patricia Hagan:

> The first peach and melon fingers of dawn began to slowly creep above the shadowy domes, spires, and crosses that made up the skyline of St. Petersburg, Russia, to stealthily push aside the clawing vestiges of night, parting the skies for a new day . . . in that late summer of 1893.

Gadzooks! "To slowly creep" and "to stealthily push aside"? Has the language so degenerated here in the Colonies that they freely split infinitives? (How can we explain to him about the starship *Enterprise*, charged "to boldly go" where no man—whoops!—no *one* has ever gone before?)

The rest seems to be Lyttonian enough. "Peach and melon fingers of dawn": more specific than "the fruity fingers of dawn" certainly. Bulwer doesn't know if he could have passed up the alliteration, though. Dawn with fingers of fruit: best not to think about that one too long. It will make some people think of sticky fingers.

What about "slowly creep"? Does anything ever creep

quickly? But these fruity fingers are pushing aside "the clawing
vestiges of night." Does this work? "Vestiges" comes from a
Latin word for footprint. Don't these people get a classical
education anymore? Fingers pushing aside clawing footprints?
She must mean that night has feet with big claws. That makes
sense. Then along comes dawn with its sweet-smelling fruity
fingers and pushes aside these smelly, clawed feet—or at least
paws over their tracks.

Then there are "the domes, spires, and crosses that made
up the skyline of St. Petersburg, Russia." Of course. The
trick is still to use more words. No use in saying "the domes,
spires, and crosses of St. Petersburg" (the domes and spires
probably rule out St. Petersburg, Florida). And then "in that
late summer of 1893." It reads like an afterthought, but this
was the last chance to throw it in. It's now or never, even if
it is placed in the emphatic final position that writers often
like to save for something of major importance. It was nice,
though, to be reminded that dawn "parts the sky" for a new
day. We might forget when dawn comes.

And look! There is not a person in sight to distract us. The
stage is empty. The actors (and human interest) will have to
wait to make an entrance. Bulwer thinks of his predecessor,
Walter Scott, who set a standard for opening historical novels
in *Guy Mannering* (1815): "It was in the beginning of the month
of November, 17—, when a young English gentleman . . ."
What if the author had heeded Scott? "It was in the late
summer of 1893 when a young woman pushed open her shut-
ters to watch the sun rise over the domes, spires, and crosses
of St. Petersburg."

His self-esteem still secure, Bulwer confidently picks up
another tome, Janet Dailey's *Heiress*:

Sunlight pierced the thick canopy formed by the branching limbs of the oak trees and dappled the century-old marble monument that laid claim to this section of the Houston cemetery as the Lawson family plot.

Bulwer is relieved. He has found another word waster, another heir—or heiress—to his tradition. We have "the thick canopy formed by the branching limbs." No use in saying "the thick canopy of branching limbs," dropping "formed by." But "branching limbs." Isn't "branching limbs" what limbs do? And they are "branching limbs of oak trees." Would her readers have felt cheated if she had said that "sunlight pierced the canopy of oak trees"? That brings the word count down from fourteen to seven—almost half.

Then we get "dappled the century-old marble monument that laid claim to this section of the Houston cemetery as the Lawson family plot." Not a very economical way of saying that the sunlight is falling on the Lawson family plot. And in the next sentence she again tells the reader that the marble had been cut over a hundred years earlier to watch over the graves of the first Lawsons. Why say the same thing again in slightly different words? She could have used that next sentence for some fresh information, perhaps mentioning the detail about Houston.

Now what do we have? "Sunlight pierced the canopy of oak trees and dappled the century-old monuments of the Lawson family plot." Nah. You can't write like that and extrude one 500-page novel after another.

Bulwer is on a roll. He snatches up Gail Godwin's *A Southern Family*:

Going to see Clare's family on the isolated hilltop where Ralph Quick had built his domestic fortress was an ordeal for Julia.

Bulwer can sympathize with the ordeal, having his own of wading through a seventeen-word subject phrase before a verb finally surfaces. And what a verb to wait for: *was*. Not exactly kinetic, much less melodramatic. A lot of sentences like to build to some kind of conclusion, to some highlight. At least we get Julia, though, even if she sounds a trifle petulant. Having to go see the relatives in their isolated hilltop fortress is bad enough, but being asked to hold up the ends of anticlimactic sentences would try the patience of any Southern belle.

"Going to see." Doesn't that mean "visiting"? And Ralph Quick? Sounds like a bounder. A proper Victorian gentleman would have a name like . . . like Nigel Pangbourne. But Julia's okay. Half the heroines in Victorian novels are named Julia or Emily.

But how can we get some interest and climax into that opener and allow a lady of quality her rightful precedence? There must be a way. Let's try "It was always an ordeal for Julia to visit Clare's family on the isolated hilltop where Ralph Quick had built his domestic fortress." This structure begins by positing the ordeal: "It was always an ordeal . . ." What was an ordeal? "For Julia to visit etc." Question raised, question answered. Furthermore, the sentence ends climactically with the imposing image of the domestic fortress.

Bulwer enjoys his vindication. Who are these colonial upstarts to impugn his literary honor? He seizes *The Sins of the Flesh*, by Fern Michaels:

The night was womblike with a dense, cloudy sky hanging overhead as if suspended.

"Womblike"—he doesn't even want to think about that one. In his day only expectant ladies, midwives, and physicians talked about wombs. But the cloudy sky is hanging "as if suspended." This one stops him for a moment, but then he remembers the dictionaries two tables away. He picks up one and consults its definition of *hang*: "to attach to something from above with no support from below; *suspend*." Ah, the clouds were suspended overhead as if suspended. Now that is emphasis. And he doesn't miss that the clouds are overhead, right where you would find them in his day. That is one thing that hasn't changed.

Bulwer likes the game. He is still a match for any of these puppies. He decides to try just one more, *The Servants of Twilight*, by Dean R. Koontz:

It began in sunshine, not on a dark and stormy night.

At last, somebody in this century who knows how to start a novel! At least if he returned he would have one peer; then he remembers his contemporary nemesis, the only novelist of his day whose works outsold his own. But Bulwer takes comfort in recollecting how he could sometimes raise a laugh by reciting one of this fellow's more self-indulgent openers:

It was the best of times, it was the worst of times, it was the age of wisdom, it was the age of foolishness, it was the epoch of belief, it was the epoch of incredulity . . .

Indeed. It would have been so much easier to say "It was a dark and stormy age."

1988 WINNER

Like an expensive sports car, fine-tuned and well-built, Portia was sleek, shapely and gorgeous, her red jumpsuit molding her body, which was as warm as the seatcovers in July, her hair as dark as new tires, her eyes flashing like bright hubcaps, and her lips as dewy as the beads of fresh rain on the hood; she was a woman driven—fueled by a single accelerant—and she needed a man, a man who wouldn't shift from his views, a man to steer her along the right road, a man like Alf Romeo.
                                                —*Rachel E. Sheeley*
                                                      Williamsburg, Ind.

1989 WINNER

Professor Frobisher couldn't believe he had missed seeing it for so long—it was, after all, right there under his nose—but in all his years of research into the intricate and mysterious ways of the universe, he had never noticed that the freckles on his upper lip, just below and to the left of the nostril, partially hidden until now by the hairy mole he had just removed a week before, exactly matched the pattern of the stars in the Pleiades, down to the angry red zit that had just popped up where he and his colleagues had only today discovered an exploding nova.
                                                —*Ray C. Gainey*
                                                      Indianapolis, Ind.

1990 WINNER

Dolores breezed along the surface of her life like a flat stone forever skipping across smooth water, rippling reality sporadically but oblivious to it consistently, until she finally lost momentum, sank and, due to an overdose of fluoride as a child which caused her to suffer from chronic apathy, doomed herself to lie forever on the floor of her life as useless as an appendix and as lonely as a five-hundred-pound barbell in a steroid-free fitness center. —*Linda Vernon*
Newark, Calif.

1991 WINNER

Sultry it was and humid, but no whisper of air caused the plump, laden spears of golden grain to nod their burdened heads as they unheedingly awaited the cyclic rape of their gleaming treasure, while overhead the burning orb of luminescence ascended its ever-upward path toward a sweltering celestial apex, for although it is not in Kansas that our story takes place, it looks godawful like it. —*Judy Frazier*
Lathrop, Mo.

LYTTONY I

The hair ball blocking the drain of the shower reminded
Laura she would never see her little dog Pritzi again.
—*Claudia J. Fields*
Santa Barbara, Calif.

It could have been an organically based disturbance of the
brain—perhaps a tumor or a metabolic deficiency—but after
a thorough neurological exam it was determined that Byron
was simply a jerk.
—*Jeffrey C. Jahnke*
McMinnville, Oreg.

While the luminescent moon swelled in the sky like the
bloated belly of a tuna, Michael, sitting on the deck of his
large yacht, stared at the rolling waves and remembered the
last time he had seen Greta, her lacy pink dress besmirched
with a blob of chocolate ice cream, her black patent leather
shoes still shiny, as he made a tearful farewell and sold her
for medical experiments to the university's primate institute.
—*Kelly J. Messinger*
Huntington, W. Va.

"The show must go on! Harry would have wanted it that way!" Nick sobbed over the slain musician's casket, but privately, in the deep orchestral recesses of his mind, he pondered—would 75 trombones indeed be enough to lead the big parade?
                                        —*Bill Linden*
                                        Park Ridge, Ill.

Nothing ever made me madder than coming home to find my pet python's throat slit—all the way down.
                                        —*Scott Slemmons*
                                        Lubbock, Tex.

Everyone west of the Pecos knew that Long Jim Strood was wanted for cattle rustling, a noise he produced by rubbing two steers together.
                                        —*John Kolm*
                                        East Melbourne, Australia

"I wouldn't advise ya to be amblin' out there, ma'am," drawled Tex, inclining his weathered features toward the hostile, forbidding desert behind them which stretched on and on unceasingly in the distance, dotted only with an occasional yucca or bleached bison bones (which had their own story to tell of how the West was won in this harshly unforgiving landscape), "on account of them In'juns."
                                        —*Merrielle Turnbull*
                                        Las Vegas, Nev.

Bruce, who was disconsolate as he watched the flames licking at his beloved forest, winced when he saw the flashes of light and heard the soft, furry detonations of the koala bears, soaked inside and out with the volatile eucalyptus oil that gave them life, and then, alas, sealed their fiery fate, but thank

God Sheila was there to remind him, "Life's a bitch, mate, and then you explode!"
                                      —*Gale Myers*
                                      Honolulu, Hawaii

"Since marriage is not to be leapt into, I know I must kiss a few frogs before finding my prince; but if this goes on much longer, I think I'll croak," pondered Lady Fernbrake as Baronet Robert Ribbett kissed her so long and deep she gasped for breath, her breast heaving like the throat sacs of twin tree toads.
                                      —*Greg Oehme*
                                      Grass Valley, Calif.

Shading her eyes against the dark, she peered through the early light of dawn as it filtered into the forest, seeking some sign of her departed lover, who just last night had promised his return before the sun should rise to its noonday apex, when she heard the muffled sound of rustling wings above her and looking upward saw the soft brown eyes of her beloved staring at her with longing from the face of a spotted magenta moth, rubbing its many legs together in a plaintive courting song, striking terror to the marrow of her bones, as she gasped, "My God, he's pupated!"
                                      —*Barbara Cleaver Kroll*
                                      Kennett Square, Pa.

Stanley looked quite bored and somewhat detached, but then penguins often do.
                                      —*John Witschey*
                                      Alexandria, Va.

Ralph, feeling deeply the responsibility of being the sole remaining guardian of the sanctity of animal rights at the entrance to the nightclub at 4:00 A.M. in the morning, could naught but swing mightily his bucket of red paint—ersatz

blood, the real thing having curdled hours before—at the extremely tall lady in a fur coat (actually, considering how it rose majestically over her head and fell smoothly to ground level, almost a coverall), although he began to realize, when the fanged, red-eyed creature turned angrily in his direction, that the moon was full, he was alone on Park Avenue, and he had better haul ass.   —*G. L. Goe*
Greenwood, Ind.

"Sex is all I ever seem to think about," grumbled Humphry as he turned from the freshly dug grave, wiped the loose dirt from his hands and knees, and leaned against the lurid neon sign proclaiming "*SAM'S CEMETERY—YOUR PUTREFAC-TION GUARANTEED*" to smoke a stale cigarette while casually stomping a rat.   —*Amy Woodward*
Hingham, Mass.

The evilly gibbous moon shed its leering light upon the moor and the running figure of Ronald Brownley, who—with hands clutching the forbidden amulet and ears filled with the hellish ululation of thousands of bounding, spectral hounds—realized that it had been he, and he alone, who'd cast the horribly portentous deciding vote against the town's leash law.
—*Joette M. Rozanski*
Toledo, Ohio

Like an overripe beefsteak tomato rimmed with cottage cheese, the corpulent remains of Santa Claus lay dead on the hotel floor.
—*John Renfro Davis*
Conroe, Tex.

I looked out over the dark city, and the twinkling lights reminded me of the glint from my mother-in-law's tooth.
—*James P. Caron*
Denver, Colo.

Looking for all the world like a gigantic celestial coffee ring, the crescent moon sloshed its feeble light upon the greasy tablecloth of the night sky.
—*Karen S. Garvin*
College Park, Md.

Escaping the prison farm and fleeing headlong through the tickling tendrils of the swamp's luxuriant, overripe foliage, I realized that in the great scheme of things the fetid odor of the bayou's primordial ooze, while more desirable than the staccato bark of the guard's primordial Uzi, was not as attractive as the prospect of lying in the arms of Sarah Mae, my primordial floozy, or as satisfying as the thought of swilling from a bottle of Old Rotgut, my primordial booze.

—*Calvin Cahan*
Austin, Tex.

The silent snow fell relentlessly, unceasingly, mercilessly from the sordid, sullied surreality of the sky as if some enormous, ethereal diner were shaking grated Parmesan on the great soggy meatball that was Earth.   —*Joan Mazulewicz*
Liverpool, N.Y.

The sun peered over the eastern horizon like a voyeuristic Cyclops, lasciviously ogling the Earth, which was still clad in the diaphanous, dew-speckled garb that is Mother Nature's nightie.   —*Cora Williams Weisenberger*
Richton Park, Ill.

Seeing the unoccupied taxi, he bolted across the street, bolted like cabbage in the fall, bolted like rhubarb before he got a chance to make jam, bolted like lightning in the heat of a summer storm, bolted like his back door to keep out prowlers, bolted to the floor like his desk in the first grade, but missed it anyway, which drove him nuts, like the pecans in his pie on Christmas, like the almonds ground in his chocolate torte, like the filberts in fruitcake, like the chunky peanut butter on his English muffin, like the little metal round things screwed tightly on all his bolts.   —*Susan A. Johnson*
Sunderland, Mass.

As Maria walked along the beach, the clouds grew angry, the sea raged, the wind howled, and the sand was just plain irritated.   *—Jeff Kruse*
Van Nuys, Calif.

It was a bright and windy day and puffy gray-and-white clouds bounced after the jet trail in the pale blue sky like fuzzy-wuzzy kittens chasing a long white string.
      —Janet E. Rash
Indianapolis, Ind.

In desperation, in what could become the most spectacular upset in tennis doubles' history—Magnolia Blossom and her sister Chrys (short for Chrysanthemum), who were seeded first and now only one point from losing the Floral Gardens title to Violet Primrose and her sister Daffy (short for Daffodil), who weren't seeded at all—seedless, one might say—Magnolia slammed the tennis ball over the taut tendrils of the net directly at Daffodil, but Daffy ducked, and the crowd gasped as the bulbous ball butted by her, until Violet raced in, tightly gripping the long stem of her racket, smacked the sucker crosscourt, planting it beyond her opponents' reach, and nipping the match-winning point in the bud.   *—Michael Savoy*
New York, N.Y.

Informed by Scotland Yard of the discovery of the bodies of Laplander frogmen in the hire of the Irish Republican Army who had been drugged with chloral hydrate in their beer, weighted down with rolls of five dollar bills and the scores of a Sibelius symphony, and then hurled from the windows of a cable railway carriage to drown in a Somersetshire swamp, the

Home Secretary mused disbelievingly, "Funicular defenestrated Fenian finned Finnis Mickey Finned; finally finished in a fen by fins and *Finlandia*."   —*Robert D. Norris, Jr.*
                                                              Tulsa, Okla.

It was an unusual sunset, with the sea sucking the sun from the sky, sort of the way a dog might suck the yolk from an egg, but not exactly.   —*Anna Jean Mayhew*
                                                              Chapel Hill, N.C.

The hail pattered against the window like popcorn popping in a well-buttered saucepan; the lightning flashed like a lightbulb when the refrigerator door is opened; the thunder rumbled distantly like a single, lonely chocolate bonbon rolling about in the cookie jar—all of these things kept Cherry awake as she tried to keep her mind off of her diet.
                                                              —*Laurie M. Tossing*
                                                              Mesa, Ariz.

The smoking volcano towered over the newly constructed Club Dread, raining unsightly black ash over the nude beach, causing the vacationing secretaries and computer programmers to bolt for the cabana, their oiled bodies collecting ebony dust as they fled, so that the assembled crowd of erstwhile sun worshipers looked like an obscene minstrel show.
                                                              —*Gregory Mast*
                                                              San Jose, Calif.

When Anastasia turned her awful glare on him, Roger's heart went into overdrive, the way the four cylinders of his '74 Ford

Pinto had labored to climb the Rocky Mountains last summer, and Roger knew their relationship was destined to end the same—in a fireball, rear-ended by fate.

—*Larry M. Brill*
Austin, Tex.

Her long, dark hair blew in the breeze, like those red, plastic flags you see rippling in the wind at a used-car dealer's lot.

—*Linda Frederick*
Union City, Calif.

Guest Entry: And then their water broke . . .
The monsoon clouds, pregnant with rain, growled and grunted across the swollen pewter sky. The dome of afternoon pressed down on the earth like a soggy blanket, trapping the oppressive humidity and laying low even the most fortitudinous, their bodies robbed of energy and their minds of will.

—*Best-selling Historical Romance*

Wisconsin Bob was a little bit of Nevada Smith, Rhode Island Red, brothers Indiana and Kentucky Jones, Duncan Idaho, Joe Montana, Tennessee Williams, and Oklahoma Crude all rolled into one; and his was a precious state, as at the moment Minnesota Fats stood over him, an Alaskantine menace, poised to jump and squash him like an Oregon blueberry; but, not untypically, his mind was not on the Texas-sized problem before him, rather his thoughts were on his two Maine gals: a Georgia peach named Carolina Washington, a vision of Southern pulchritude in her New Jersey dress; and last but not least, Virginia Penn, New York cheesecake,

topped with the innocence of a Kansas wheat field, with long, long (we're talkin' LONG) legs that look like they could stretch all the way from New Mexico to Florida—with Mississippi burning in between.   —*Jim Horn*
                                       Portland, Oreg.

VILE PUNS

> **Writing Tip #3**   There is no substitute for curiosity to keep the reader involved. The reader should constantly be asking questions, like "What is going on here?" "What did she mean by that remark?" "Isn't he acting out of character?" and "Why did I buy this book?"

Among us comedy writers, the pun is considered the lowest form of humor and a sure sign of burnout, which is why when I tried to sneak one by, my associates had me committed to the Institute for Disturbed Comic Writers at Vail, Colorado— so I now know why they say "Use a pun, go to Vail!"

—*Robert M. Quan*
San Francisco, Calif.

"Mine! All mine!!" cried the lost Dutchman, assaying his prospects of striking gold with that new dancehall girl, Molly B. Denim, the one who led the dancers, who, while a minor, had a bronzed body and a brassy attitude, and would've meddled in his affairs except that he yelled, "Iron my clothes!" and she yelled back, "It'll take a cop or two to make me!" and he steeled himself (having a fine mettle) and yelled back, "Nick'll do it!" and she suggested, "Ore . . ." but got cut off by a pewtered miner (who obviously wanted to drill her) who asked, "You vant me? I zinc so!" and she knew she'd gotten the shaft.

—*David Edward Nale*
Houston, Tex.

The burly new students at Dan's All-Male Toe-Dance-A-Torium teetered nervously against the wall, as their instructor intoned, "Ballet up to the barre, boys!"

—*Lynne Marie Waldron*
Campbell, Calif.

His eyes were like an unfurled tape measure, taking in her considerable physical attributes, and "Sew!" he said to her, needling her with every word, "it seams you have been feeling hemmed in lately," and she could see the pattern of her life clearly now because what he said had a trace of truth in it, and she stood there facing him, hoping he would lay her down and press her to him, as his eyes darted to her fully dressed form, fashioning a fantasy, his mind tailoring the right words to fit the situation; instead, he kept her in stitches all night.

—*Estelle Brundige*
Schenectady, N.Y.

Michael brought a small butter knife and a tub of margarine into his tiny room, removed his shirt, and patted himself on the back.

—*Kenneth Leffler*
Falls Church, Va.

Since the recently discovered home movies of Adolf Hitler's summer vacation in his recreational vehicle were untitled, it was decided to call them *Mein Kampfer.*

—*Ron Reinhold*
Phoenix, Ariz.

It was a dark and stormy Arabian night, not unlike a thousand others, and though jarred by forty heaves the seasick

sailor, Ali, babbled on, sharpening his scimitar by lamplight and exclaiming to the wealthy merchant of Baghdad, "I am a lad in need of a nest egg, Sinbad, and I am going to get a piece of the roc!"
                                          —*John L. Ashman*
                                          Houston, Tex.

After escaping from a derailed circus train, the big cat approached the city slowly and cautiously, scratching suburban fences while exploring backyards and befouling children's sandboxes, prompting the local tabloid to blare the warning headline "Sandy Claws Is Coming to Town!"
                                          —*Rich Chadwin, M.D.*
                                          Porterville, Calif.

The arrow flew through the air like a pigeon bound for home, and, as it buried itself in the chest of the shafted late Earl of Abercrombie, Robert, who had let fly without a quiver, decided that in no possible way could William tell who had done the deed.
                                          —*Alison Hall*
                                          Ottawa, Ontario

Although Sarah had an abnormal fear of mice, it did not keep her from eeking out a living at a local pet store.
                                          —*Richard W. O'Bryan*
                                          Perrysburg, Ohio

"My wife is gone, gone, never to return!" cried Mr. Westheimer ruthlessly.
                                          —*Elizabeth Ivanovich*
                                          Watsonville, Calif.

As Mick Jagger's personal orthopedist, Frank had a long and successful career which reached its high point when the rock star's leg broke and he alone was able to cast the first Stone.
—Jeffrey Anbinder
Henry Bial
Dobbs Ferry, N.Y.

Dr. Maurice "Mo" Portajohn, surgeon for a small group of Texans in San Antonio, packed his surgical kit with diuretics, laxatives, and astringents in anticipation of an upcoming battle with the Mexican Army, and as he shut the valise and walked through the door of his adobe hovel that had been home for the past three years, he heard his wife, Hepatica, call, "You forgot the alum, Mo!"
—Bill Reeves
Reno, Nev.

Peterbilt Trucks—aren't we all, in a manner of speaking, Peterbilt Trucks?
—W. R. C. Shedenhelm
Ventura, Calif.

He died as he had lived, a dirt-poor but happy farmer, Mother Nature's caretaker in the heartland of America, and now as his son, Bud, listened to the reading of his father's will, bequeathing his last earthly possession, a female sheep, he could hear his father's pun-loving voice resounding in the lawyer's reading of "This ewe's for Bud."
—Jack Markov
Philadelphia, Pa.

Father William "Tiny" O'Flaherty raised himself to his full height of four feet eleven inches and, peering myopically at the assembled congregation of two nuns, Flynn the verger, old Mrs. McSweeney, and the cat from the Presbyterian church down the road, mused that it was not for nothing that he was known as Small Denominational Bill.

—*Alison Hall*
Ottawa, Ontario

Gloria was a woman of violent contrasts: her navel—white, soft, and desirable—was an innie, while her car—black, swift, and powerful—was an Audi. —*Brian W. Holmes*
San Jose, Calif.

"My left eye has been slowly shifting over to the right side of my face!" she floundered. —*Trevor Dennie*
Gloversville, N.Y.

Van der Koff hawked and spit onto the canvas; yes, the world would soon hear of the Phlegmish painters.

—*John Gahl*
Winsted, Conn.

A grubby little street urchin, he would often be found scrounging for leftovers in darkened movie houses and, thus, was known to many as the Popcorn Pauper.

—*Leslie Bruce*
Vermilion, Alberta

LAST NIGHT
I DREAMT I
WENT TO
MANDERLY
AGAIN

Last night I dreamt I went to Manderly again, where I had first arrived a shy bride (and departed a woman), cowed by the psychotic housekeeper Mrs. Danvers (who expired dramatically when she set fire to the west wing), and haunted by Maxim's first wife, Rebecca, whom I thought Maxim still loved (except he never had, and who took her own life in such a way as to make it look as though Maxim had murdered her)— but stop!—I'm getting ahead of my story.

—*Jean B. Brownell*
Portland, Oreg.

Night's ominous blackness rolled across the city of London as the banshee death wail of the air-raid siren summoned the populace to be swallowed into the labyrinthine bowels of the Underground as if the earth were a giant mouth sucking up so many strands of spaghetti; meanwhile, in America, a birth occurred which, twenty years later, would prove that neither of these events had any connection whatsoever.

—*P. A. Lamers*
Wilmington, Del.

Baltimore—port city to the world—Fort McHenry—"The Star-Spangled Banner"—the Inner Harbor—Edgar Allan Poe—Babe Ruth—steamed crabs—lacrosse at Homewood Field—marble steps . . . but this has nothing to do with our story, *Twilight in Boise.* —*Mike Marucci*
Dundalk, Md.

The searing white disk of the sun drove daggers into his heat-maddened brain, scorching and scouring all thought, all memory, leaving him finally just a dry husk of a man with no recollection of green English fields, rippling scull-dotted waters, or even pale, smooth-skinned Emma, which was scarcely strange as the poor man was a displaced Masai cattle herder. —*Zack Larner*
Bonny Doon, Calif.

As I look back over all the loves of my life, none were so overpowering as that of Clark, the boy in my seventh-grade English class, whose eyes were as green as the swimming pool my mother had installed the summer before she was put in the wheelchair, and was thus too preoccupied to concern herself with its general maintenance. —*Theresa Ambrose*
Holliston, Mass.

The sun beat down hard on the Great Sahara, so hard that you could see the heat rising in columns off the solid, packed ground; and swarms of tiny rodents and other such undesirables scurrying futilely, without avail, diving for the slightest bit of shade like panicked moviegoers in a burning theater; and even the mighty cacti sweltering sweatingly in the roasting air—however, none of this is important as of yet, because

Hubert was still in Toledo waiting for the bus, which as usual was running way behind schedule.   —*Elizabeth Fekete*
                                                                                Yardley, Pa.

"Tap tap tap, tap tap tap, tap tap tap!" sounded the fury of Candice's impatience as it thundered through the tip of her perfectly manicured nail onto the cold glass cosmetics counter, but to the idiot salesclerk it signified nothing.

                                                                —*Geoffrey Eisen*
                                                                Honolulu, Hawaii

The stiletto-slit body of a woman lay sprawled on the floor, emptied and as gray and cold as steel, her eyes wide and blank and looking upward as if to follow the path of her freed though tortured soul, her feet tangled and facing south where she was born during a hurricane that nearly wiped out the entire orange crop and sent frozen juice prices soaring so high that nearly half of the nation's children had to forgo their main source of Vitamin C, though a widespread epidemic of scurvy was nipped in the bud by the hurried production of chewable tablets put out by a company in Secaucus, and she was one of those saved.   —*Doris Licameli*
                                                                Fairview, N.J.

"What's another word for 'thesaurus'?" exclaimed Beth as she thumbed through one of those books that give other words which mean the same as the one word you don't want to use again.   —*Christian M. Tessier*
                                                                Cohoes, N.Y.

Although she had known—well, not so much "known" as simply hopped into bed with—countless men, she had never—perhaps "never" is not the accurate term, her memory being rather like that kitchen utensil you place vegetables in so you can wash off insect body parts and films of pesticides without all the produce splooshing down the monstrous drain—encountered a man as tender—of course I mean "tender" figuratively, sort of like having a gentle manner and a compassionate heart and not at all like a good cut of dead calf—as Barry, and she guessed that, as long as she lived—and probably even after—she never would again.

—*Shannon Bayless*
Piedmont, Okla.

She sat with growing anger and fingernails on the concrete waiting benches in the small airport terminal, finally realizing that she was going to miss the entire Grubs and Nutrition Conference opening day ceremonies, as she heard a soothing voice coming out of the loudspeaker, "We think Flight 3 should be here pretty soon, we're sorry for any inconvenience that this delay may have caused, and finally we here at Godot Airlines appreciate your patience!"   —*Paul Streeter*
Novato, Calif.

"Because so many readers write in when we do, we will *never* end a sentence with a preposition in this paper!" expostulated Senior Editor Percy Whyte, causing cub reporter Willy Watson to ruminate ponderingly, "Well, of course I would never use a preposition to finish a sentence up with, because it might be difficult to make sense out of, and, after all, what would I want to use a preposition to finish a sentence that you cannot make any sense out of up with for?"

—*Robert Lodge*
Seattle, Wash.

"Heavens!" groaned fair Diana Rea (a groan uttered to the heights from her depths as she strained every muscle of her viscera (her bowel, her gut, her innermost being (that from which the great sages have mined their deepest wisdom (unlike middling ones, who only mine the mind (though Diana had quite a lucid mind in her lovely head (which sat on small, soft shoulders over which cascaded mounds of flaming red hair (if one may say mounds cascade (or that red hair flames, for that matter, though well it seemed to on Diana (who, though pretty, wasn't shallow, but contemplated life's landscape in its heights and depths, lights and darks (like Kierkegaard, whom she was reading at the time (though *nausea* was the *opposite* of *her* problem)))))))))), "I *do* wish I could get over this constipation thing, but I must admit that the time I've spent on the pot reading has worked wonders for my knowledge of the humanities."
                                                    —*Greg Oehme*
                                                    Grass Valley, Calif.

Lyle's face could communicate much in a single expression, and as he stood in my doorway, he had that I-got-a-great-deal-on-some-Jets-tickets-but-I-need-fifty-bucks-right-away-because-the-guy-with-the-tickets-is-double-parked-downstairs-and-he's-in-a-big-hurry-because-he-thinks-the-Samoan-Mafia-is-after-him-but-he's-really-an-OK-guy-because-we-were-in-high-school-together-and-that-parole-violation-was-only-a-sneaky-technicality-so-can-I-have-the-money-right-away look.
                                                    —*Mark Biscuso*
                                                    Eagen, Minn.

"I have had enough," he shouted, bringing his hand down with a loud smack on the dining room table, causing that usually brave structure to tremble, which set all the cake plates

and coffee cups and saucers quivering and made the Little Boy Blue and Little Bo-Peep salt and pepper shakers shiver and move slightly nearer to each other, as if for reassurance, while a tiny drop of wax fell like a baby tear from the plump little candle in its snug holder, "of all this anthropomorphizing!"
—*Kimberly Larsen*
Beaverton, Oreg.

A whimper escaped her pouting lips as the sadistic yet gentle Marquess of Derrywood pulled her resisting yet somewhat willing, slender yet voluptuous body, slowly yet inevitably and forcefully yet tenderly toward his powerful yet restrained body and whispered hoarsely yet mellifluously, "I love no other woman but you, Evangeline . . . tonight."
—*Susan Ko*
Fremont, Calif.

Our story commences with an account of the ghoulish death of the Duke of Breathwaite which, although of little importance to the main events unfolding herein, establishes the atmosphere quite nicely.
—*Michael Haynes*
Lantz, Nova Scotia

Her pallid hands hung quietly by her sides like dead ptarmigans, fluttering up to her face in dovelike motions whenever he spoke to her, then coming to rest on his hot forehead like albino pigeons that deposited little gifts of cool caresses, all the while chirping away about the day's events while his ex-wife looked at her like a snake that had just seen its first bird.
—*Carla Mathews*
Livermore, Calif.

LYTTONY II

> **Writing Tip #5: Visualization** Your readers will need help visualizing your characters. Give them all the help they need. Be generous with details. Don't leave your readers with a lot of filling-in to do. If they want to use their imaginations, let them write their own damned books.

Amanda-June kept pencil leads in her empty earring holes for two reasons.
—*Wayne Shannon*
Fort Lee, N.J.

Wilbur Johnson, a farmer, a man of courage and gentle wisdom, a man with his feet planted four-square in the furrows of life, started this day as any day, but was oblivious to the John Deere of destiny inexorably bearing down upon him.
—*Richard Manny*
Dana Kober-Manny
Tampa, Fla.

It was a typical late August afternoon in South Georgia, Orville reflected: Mam and the baby, both filmed with sweat generated from the humidity; Johnson covered with whittlin' shavings; Meemaw, chin against chest, adrift in a dementia-induced doze; and Lena picking at the garden dirt under her toenails with a splinter from the porch rail.
—*Jackie Baird*
Powell, Tenn.

The twin boys hung like wet wash on the limbs of the fat oak tree and for hours they took turns betting on whose saliva would spiral down to the earth the fastest.

—_Beth Mart_
New York, N.Y.

As the pickup truck swerved off the dirt road and rumbled end over end, real slow, just like in those movies on cable TV, Mike saw his life passing before his eyes, also real slow, like those slow-motion special effects things in the movies, except that his life was not all that interesting, and he thought (although he couldn't be sure) that he saw some parts of it twice just to fill in the long, slow free-fall before the truck landed, on its wheels, in the soft muck of the river bottom, leaving him to live what would become a far more interesting life.

—_Barbara Forsberg Buckley_
Acton, Mass.

In her later years, Great-Grandma would point a bony finger at the aged saber above the mantle and spin long tales of how her Uncle Isaac had snatched it from a Yankee colonel's hand on the fierce, bloody field at Chickamauga, even though we all knew the closest Uncle Ike had ever come to combat had been in fighting flies while digging latrines and that the sword came into the family years after the War, purchased for $12 from an Atlanta pawnshop; still, we let her prattle on, partly out of our near-Oriental Southern respect for ancestors, but mainly because the doddering matriarch controlled a tobacco fortune worth just over $87 million.

—_David Willingham_
Georgetown, Tenn.

When she saw what she had done, Willa's face turned as white as the bleached belly of a whale that had lain in the sun for days and withered from the heat, then had expanded again, larger, with the fermenting, liquefying gases of death.
—*Elaine C. Smith*
Tallahassee, Fla.

Pondering her predicament, Susie Jo-Ellen could sense a solution forming in the back of her mind, but getting it to the front of her mind was like the long, slow, twisting, tortuous journey of water through the corroded, mineral-encrusted, lime-laced West Texas water pipes, and like the water, when it finally got there, it was no good.   —*Pam N. Shurley*
San Angelo, Tex.

It was a whelming sight to see the diverse and varied myriads of the chronologically gifted, persons of color, those with various sexual preferences, the impaired, the gender-determined, the political party strategists and IRS officials as they deplaned to network and empower one another while they decried discrimination and the demise of the English language.
—*Craig D. Anderson*
San Jose, Calif.

Maria was quite mortified when the crack Vatican investigation squad dispatched to her home ruled that the wondrous reflection off her new toaster was a coincidence rather than a true miracle, even though deep in her heart she too had wondered why in heaven's name the amazingly detailed image depicted our Savior wearing a Van Halen T-shirt and a crown

of safety pins while playing air guitar in a vat of French poo-
dles, rather than a more traditional scene.   —*Richard Carter*
Hampton, Va.

When Dirk Pitcairn, the wildly handsome, rippling-muscled
outlaw of the outback, crushed me in his arms, bent me over
backward, and murmured, "Little one, Little one!" all the
while his fevered lips searing my cheek like a midwest com-
bine in a Kansas wheat field, I said, "Sir, if you will allow me
to straighten up, I think you will find I am every bit as tall as
you are."   —*Mary B. Bradford*
Easton, Md.

"The French have a word for it," Frankie Kowalski of Pittsburgh slowly and stiffly nodded as he glared across the Somme,
for the first time fully understanding the implications of what
he was saying: "The French have a word for everything."
—*Mark Burky*
Denver, Colo.

It was one of those patient-etherized-upon-a-table kind of
evenings, Chubbly Gorillawitz mused to himself as he
crushed, with the lackadaisical zeal that had always charac-
terized the Gorillawitz clan, another empty Schlitz can against
the gentle slope of his oft-furrowed brow.
—*Peter Uhlman*
Stephen Heuser
New Haven, Conn.

THE WAY
WE LIVE NOW

Writing Tip #6: Getting Ideas   There are lots of swell ideas for novels that no one has exhausted yet. What about a womanizing British agent (you could change his nationality) with a license to kill, or—better yet—a love story about a couple who originally disliked one another, or—even better than that—a police thriller about two incompatible partners, one a cynical, street-wise veteran and the other an eager, by-the-books rookie?

Many men had tried to tame Rosalita of the Flashing Eyes, whose wild beauty had made feverish their dreams and restless their waking hours, yet she was as willful as she was beautiful and cared nothing for their rough begging, their extravagant gifts bought with last dollars; she wanted only to be on "Wheel of Fortune" and to fold like a soft tortilla into the arms of Pat Sajak.
          —*Leslie Riley Cannon*
          Cincinnati, Ohio

She picked up her pen and held it as if it were covered with toe jam while the sweat of her brow trickled down her cheeks to mingle with the salty warmth of her tears, the trembling of her hand indicative of the cold in her heart, as though night crawlers had eaten through her soul and wormed their way into her thoughts, as was the case every time she tried to write Arsenio.
          —*Patty Teubert*
          Beckley, W.Va.

Sigmund realized he'd better stop playing with the cat: the interviewers, seeing his horribly scratched arms and hands, would think he was a junkie, and he'd never get into med school.
—*Charles Hamilton*
Baltimore, Md.

Just in the nick of time, Dr. Gillespie remembered the insistent lecturing of his old surgery professor: a surgeon must never say, "Oops!"; a surgeon should always say, "There!"
—*Melanie Nickel*
San Diego, Calif.

Gretel the scrub nurse smiled secretly to herself beneath her stiff green mask when she heard the satisfactory "thwap!" of the scalpel as she delivered it neatly into the taut gloved hand of the surgeon (before he even had a chance to ask for it) and raising her eyes to meet his for one gaze-locked moment it seemed that time had stood still, except that time hadn't stood still and when a pungent odor wafted into their slightly flared nostrils their eyes dropped in horror to see that he had neglected to turn off the cauterizing instrument and there was now a hole the size of a Matanuska cabbage in the patient's spleen.
—*Laura A. Campbell*
Anchorage, Ala.

I'll never forget how their rheumy old eyes lit up with joy when I told them they could come to live with me instead of spending their last days in the poorhouse, or how their bony jaws fell to their chests after they came here and realized that

if they wanted one good meal a day and a cot to collapse on at night, they'd better work their damn butts off or else.
—*Phoebe Weiss*
Nazareth, Pa.

From the crest of the hill, John gazed down upon the little seaport town—fir trees poking through the morning fog; a heron gliding over the marshlands; the ornate Victorian court-house like a gaudy brooch on the bosom of a dignified spinster; the sailboats bobbing at the dock as the wind slapped the halyards against their masts: *spink, spink, spelank*—and thought, "What a place to build a McDonald's!"
—*Patricia Spaeth*
Port Townsend, Wash.

The baseball, seemingly with an inertia of its own, shot like a cat from a cannon, rocketing from home plate and crashing through the billboard on the centerfield fence displaying the woman holding the pack of Salems who had once been the mayor of Billings, and thusly slowed just enough so that it securely settled on the back seat of the Suzuki Samurai which paused before, but did not turn into, the garish but architec-turally ambivalent Pup'n Taco.
—*Paul Streeter*
Novato, Calif.

Maybe it was Al Capone's tomb, or maybe it was his com-plete lack of objectivity, but something told me Geraldo Rivera was bad news.
—*Cora Williams Weisenberger*
Richton Park, Ill.

Lance was passing Pittsburgh for the second time as his window washer fluid ran dry, leaving the wipers to etch murky

rainbows of mud, sand, and salt on the outside of his wind-shield as his frustration fogged the inside, when he finally decided to throw his Rustoleum-Red 1972 VW Bug into reverse in one last desperate attempt to disassociate its front bumper from the rear of an overly efficient and speeding highway salt spreader while there was still enough time to get to Sasha's New Year's Eve party where he intended to maneuver close enough to Guinevere at the stroke of midnight to finally get the kiss he'd dreamed of since last New Year's when a similiar predicament kept him on the road past dawn and into the worst parts of Scranton.   —*Thomas G. Cataldo*
                                              Savage, Md.

Young Lily Chrysanthemum glowed as radiantly as the mid-day sun in her lacy white gown on this beautiful summer's day; and as the doors standing in front of her opened wide as if by some heavenly power, the music from within embraced her ears and reminded the slightly dizzy Lily exactly where she was and what must be done; and so she stepped inside and began her journey down the aisle, her eyes gazing down-ward all the while, and after what seemed an eternity, reached the aisle's end and stopped, lifting her head ever so slightly to clearly hear the man, whose words, undoubtedly recited many times before, seemed to emanate from God himself: "Attention, K-Mart shoppers!" and with that she squatted and slung a twenty-five-pound bag of fertilizer over her shoulder.
                                              —*Greg Stacy*
                                              Hillsborough, Calif.

The mother of the bride sat in rapturous relief, thoughts tumbling through her head like thundering bowling balls, watching her only daughter, her darling Daphne, being united in holy wedlock, recalling how this child of hers had so many times courted disaster, being wooed and bedded by a series of manipulative, felonious deceivers—politicians, cabinet-members, drug peddlers, stockbrokers—but who, through the grace of God, had come to safe harbor, had at last found an unsullied mate—a TV evangelist.

—Barbara Cleaver Kroll
Kennett Square, Pa.

It was his bark, and not his bite, that grabbed hold of my attention as if it were a bone, preventing me from pulling away, as the sound of poor little Fluffy choking on the chicken bone came into my mind, bringing up all the wonderful memories of our time together, until I could lurch away past the cockatoos, cats, and cash register, out of the petshop and into the relative emotional emptiness of the mall.

—Dick Pasky
Willis, Mich.

Imagine Prunella Spinster's delight when, as President of the three-member local chapter of the Audubon Society, she received a second call from the large man with the cigar asking if she would be willing to demonstrate her bird-calling talents for a little documentary film he was making at the quaint coastal village of Bolinas. *—Don Roberts*
Orinda, Calif.

"Definitely an assertive wine, perhaps even aggressive, yet with a touch of whimsey," mused Professor Cartwright thoughtfully as one tentacle of the viscous purple fluid thrust him into the biolab's giant wine press while another sliced cheese and a third laid out crackers and wheat thins.

—*R. Carter*
Brookfield, Ill.

Betty Lou paused in vigorously pulling and squeezing the old cow's udders and caressingly ran her fingers over the smooth, hard metal surface of her milking pail, dreaming lustily as she did so of cousin Zeke's new pectoral implants, paid for by the sale of the family tractor.

—*Michelle Aubertin*
Timmins, Ontario

A GUN IS
NOTHING BUT
A TWO-EDGED
SWORD

Even though the hatchet men were holding a gun over his head, Harry knew that a gun was nothing but a two-edged sword liable at any moment to turn its back on the very hand that was biting it.
—*Tom Whissen*
Dayton, Ohio

Fingers of lightning goosed the sphincter of night, and below, the streets of Cleveland began their peristaltic movement toward the witching hour.
—*Enid Shomer*
Peg Libertus
Gainesville, Fla.

Lightning scratched an angry finger across the gray chalkboard of the stormy summer sky, briefly illuminating the heavens, as if God had opened the refrigerator of the universe and found nothing but the sour milk, moldy cheese, and the little aluminum foil ball that's been there for so long no one remembers what's inside, and, in disgust, closed it again.
—*Cora Williams Weisenberger*
Richton, Park, Ill.

Cheese again, low-fat cheese on multigrain bread again, and it seemed to him that his predictable, uninspiring lunch was a metaphor for what his life and his teaching had become, that somewhere along the line the Great Sandwich Maker had withdrawn the pickle and the relish.

> —*Anne Guarna*
> *Colonel Light Gardens,*
> *South Australia*

It was a stark and thorny night as the schizophrenic clouds drove the moon into paranoiac peekaboo, while the hangnails of the wind goosed the treetops into belly-dancing frenzy.

> —*Martha Thomson Barclay*
> *Mason City, Iowa*

Her eyes were a shimmering iridescent opaque intermingling of blue and green shades, intertwined like lovers beneath the full moon on a summer's eve at the beach before the tide falls away, leaving behind the jetsam and flotsam of dead and dying debris that combines with the salty water to give the ocean breeze its characteristic tangy smell, which is fine when one is out in the open but oppressive if it hangs on one's clothing too long.

> —*Brenda K. Ward*
> *St. Charles, Mo.*

She was good medicine for him: an aspirin for the ache of his doubt, a balm for the abrasions of his anxiety, an ointment for the hemorrhoids of his despair.

> —*Brian W. Holmes*
> *San Jose, Calif.*

Her cruel taunts exploded like a landmine in the lilacs of his love, amputating his hopes and blowing the shoe of desire

from his heart, which now fibrillated barefoot and bleeding through the jagged shrapnel of his broken dreams.
—*Marty Fleck*
Houston, Tex.

The sun, that great fluorescent scab, slowly peeled itself off the skin of the midsummer sky, oozing blood across the horizon which gradually turned brown and disappeared as the pus-yellow moon infected the night I was to propose to Marilyn.   —*Jared R. Towler*
Manchester, Conn.

The golden chariot of the sun began its race across the cerulean sky, casting its beams upon the row of neat Victorian houses which lined the street, refracting off the milk bottles upon the front porches, and transforming the contents thereof into warmish stinking clots.   —*Jesse O. Ellis*
Frankfort, Ky.

The clock struck one, and as Rodentia heard her husband drag his tired body to bed after another long night's workout in his gym, she wondered despairingly why she had ever consented to wed this animal, this brute, this ox, this insensitive, piggish boor, whose obsession with conquering clocks could only mean one thing, she realized at last—she had married a hickory dickory dock clock jock.   —*Dottie Lamson*
Lincoln, Nebr.

Randi gazed thoughtfully up at the clear night sky, an inky canvas dotted with the tiny lights of distant suns, like lint on an infinite pair of dress slacks.   —*Cora Williams Weisenberger*
Richton Park, Ill.

The mist clung to the mountain the same way a thirteen-year-old girl clings to her boyfriend, although the mountain wasn't thinking about "getting lucky." —*Richard Patching*
Calgary, Alberta

REFRESHMENT

INSPE

GOODS

MIKE
HARDWARE,
P.I.

> **Writing Tip #8: Writing Crime Thrillers**   A good detective story should get under way at once: "Now who do you suppose killed my partner?" mused Mike Hardware aloud to no one in particular, "or is it *whom* do you suppose?"—damn, he wished he'd paid closer attention to Sister Bertella in his eighth-grade grammar class.

Mike Hardware was the kind of private eye who didn't know the meaning of the word "fear," a man who could laugh in the face of danger and spit in the eye of death—in short, a moron with suicidal tendencies.
                              —*Eddie Lawhorn*
                              Huntsville, Ala.

When she walked into my office, my heart jumped into my mouth like a frog into a pond full of fly soup; her legs were as long as a seventh-inning stretch, and when she crossed them like Gregor Mendel hybridizing peas, my resolution to tell her to go away melted like a greaseball on a New York sidewalk on an August day—I was hooked like a carp with a mouthful of chicken guts.
                              —*G. L. Goe*
                              Greenwood, Ind.

The situation at the Road Hog Cafe and Truck Stop came to a head when Bubba "Mad Dog" Johnson kicked over his chair and dashed his bowl of vichyssoise to the floor while lunging across the table, the gleaming fish fork in his hand aimed at the heart of Julius "Killer" Magurk, who sat pinned to his chair by fear and a floral lobster bib.

—*Richard W. O'Bryan*
Perrysburg, Ohio

Of course Charles was charged with murder one after attempting to revive his wife, Cynthia, by using the Heimlich maneuver after she had eaten vichyssoise soup.

—*Joseph J. Welch*
St. Petersburg, Fla.

The familiar flashing red neon sign still glimmered through the rain, but that didn't make Private Eye Harvey Chase forget he was hanging from his window three floors above the pavement with twenty curious onlookers wondering why his pants were at his ankles and a rectal thermometer was still taking his temperature.

—*Jeremy Rice*
San Jose, Calif.

Diamonds, dynamite, and Dee Parkinson all came in small packages; nor did the similarity end there, for both diamonds and Dee were jewels, while Dee and dynamite were both quite forceful, and all three were remarkably bright, at least during that split-second between the instant the dynamite inside the tiny package Dee had hoped would yield a diamond ring exploded and the moment when the petite young Phi Beta Kappa's lights went out forever.

—*Bruce Goldman*
San Francisco, Calif.

"Inspector, your theory of accidental death by choking on steak is hard to swallow because the victim, you see, eschewed meat . . . it was murder!" —*Richard B. Spears*
Tulsa, Okla.

"Oh, would *The Godfather* never had been written, then I could live my life in peace!" swore Veronica, oldest surviving member and titular head of the Genitalia family, as her concrete overshoes propelled her slowly but certainly to the bottom of the ocean floor, where her appointment with the fishes was coming due. —*Larry Sherman*
Fremont, Calif.

Sgt. Tom Katt wasn't 100 percent sure of anything, but he knew something wasn't quite right when the factory foreman told him that the nightshift guard had fallen into a vat of baby oil and softened to death. —*Wayne D. Worthey*
Washington, D.C.

As the rays of sunlight danced gaily along the cobblestones of Main Street, Detective Spencer Dirk tossed aside the wretched stub of a smoldering black Havana and knelt to inspect the perfect, round hole in the foam mask as a small rivulet of blood flowed out along the snout, dripping off the shiny black nose, and pondered whether this killing was random, whether the murderer knew his victim, or, since this was Disneyland's third projectile-induced fatality this week, whether the assailant just hated large mice.
—*Rick Vetter*
Riverside, Calif.

This is the city: a soot-covered graveyard of a million vanished dreams, with fifty-story headstones rising from the dirt to cast gray shadows on the spirits of the damned; a rat-infested sewer where the law of survival is kill them before they can kill you, and don't look too close at what's on your plate because you may not like it; a gaudy, unwashed, flabby old hooker with a thousand faces, none of them presentable; a prison whose dingy corridors I've walked for seventeen long years, trying to sweep just a little of the scum and garbage off the streets—my name's Kowalksi, and I carry a broom.

—*Grant E. Hicks*
Newton, Mass.

Berger's death wasn't fair—whose ever was?—and it certainly wasn't neat—the meat grinder in the butcher shop where Berger had worked had been shut down twice before for problems with cleanliness—but Detective Sergeant Clancy had to admit that it was certainly economical in terms of interment—since Berger would fit in a moderately large shoe box now—although Berger's rabbi was a little concerned over the fact that the wag who had murdered him had also run two pounds of pork sausage through at the same time.

—*Ray C. Gainey*
Indianapolis, Ind.

Inspector Reginald Van Holmes lay sprawled in the oversized, antique, claw-footed bathtub, contemplating a piece of lint floating about in the soap scum, his stomach inflating and deflating, causing the lint blob to be temporarily beached up on the pink-skinned surface among the black bulrushes of hair, then released afloat again in a tide of bluish slime until finally caught in the crater of Van Holmes's navel just as an iridescent

bubble shot to the surface, bursting in a foul, flatulent pop at the precise instant it struck the inspector that the murderer could be none other than the Frenchman Pierre Poseure, an incurable transvestite suffering from acute narcolepsy and who this very moment was downstairs asleep in a stall of the women's restroom.
—*Roger D. Prengel*
Lacey, Wash.

"Who would want to murder Reggie Van Guilders, Inspector?" asked Boaz Z. Latchkey, principal of Edna St. Vincent Millay High School, "I don't know, who *wouldn't* want to murder a supercilious, snotty seventeen-year-old whose stated goal in life is to have Hollywood make a movie about his life in which *he* as a *teenager* is played by George Sanders?"
—*Robert D. Norris, Jr.*
Tulsa, Okla.

As I brushed my teeth that morning, there was little hint that before the day was over I was to play a pivotal role in smashing an international drug ring which had, during the previous three months, smuggled into the U.S. nearly twelve tons of uncut, high-grade Bolivian asphalt, estimated to have a value of nearly forty-seven thousand dollars on the street.
—*Brian W. Holmes*
San Jose, Calif.

With the radio squawking that a 4711 was in progress at 37th and 127th, Murphy knocked car 495 into 3rd and headed up 5th at 70, little reckoning, as he thumbed his .38, that this would be the day his number came up.
—*Richard Nelson*
Nottinghamshire, England

Detective Burke Murk lurked in the soggy bogs around Walla Walla, Washington, while the other cops talked shop at the neighborhood doughnut shop, laughing at that jerk, Murk, who, unlike the others, would not shirk his duty, but continued surveillance at the soggy bogs rather than talk shop with the cops at the doughnut shop in Walla Walla, Washington.

—*Deborah J. Nelson*
Peoria, Ill.

The tent smelled like death—a smell that Detective Joe Luger knew well but never seemed to get used to—and the sight of another clown shot right through the nose almost made him sick, but there was a job to do, after all, so he composed himself and said to his partner, "Wow, those are really big feet!"

—*Dennis McGrath*
Hazlet, N.J.

LYTTONY III

Judge Finkel had given the clown much latitude by letting him wear stilts during the trial, but when Bozo started juggling with His Honor's gavel, the judge admonished sternly, "I will not let you turn my courtroom into a circus!"

—*Barry G. Silverman*
Phoenix, Ariz.

Sitting there in the chair that had survived three of its previous owners, Mrs. Turmeric, the only witness who could help my client, resembled in shape, odor, and attitude a pile of laundry removed from the dryer too soon and left to sour in a cold, poorly ventilated room; the clashing colors, which cascaded haphazardly over her large indefinite form, suggested a load that would have been washed on the cold permanent press cycle and reminded me of my own load of wash—at that

very moment fermenting in my washer—"But on to business,"
I sighed, "my client deserves my full concentration."
                                        —*Susan Marston*
                                        Staten Island, N.Y.

"Doc," moaned Hector as he languished on the psychiatric
couch, "the most frustrating element of my amnesia is that
when I have flashes of déjà vu, I don't even know it."
                                        —*Diane Brandi*
                                        Middletown, N.J.

That scream, that howl, that final shriek just before Egbert
died: Gwendolyn had never heard anything so horrible in all
her life, but then she had never heard walnut shells in the
garbage disposal.   —*Claire Ball*
                                        Kailua, Hawaii

He was a man of principle with hair as orange as those soft
spongy cones you see lined up on the highway just before a
road worker sticks a stop sign out right in front of your car so
a bulldozer can cross the road at two miles per hour to totally
screw up your whole day.   —*June Obrochta*
                                        Pittsburg, Calif.

"There's one CEO who's getting too big for his britches!"
Warren exclaimed, mistakenly thinking the newscaster had
announced that "the Iacocca" had decreed the death of the
blasphemous author.   —*Calvin Cahan*
                                        Austin, Tex.

"No, Warden, no, not me—I don't want to fry!" screamed "Ratface" Hanratty as he rattled the bars of his cell, "but I'll bake you a mean pandowdy!" —*John L. Ashman*
Houston, Tex.

It was quite apparent from the start that Ethel, the manicurist, who cried so easily, and was so easily moved by ordinary things, would one day find her true calling in the Opera.
—*David Bornstein*
New York, N.Y.

This time, the pesky, nagging itch that Marvin felt every time he and Mandy were alone together—an itch that started south of his tripes and spread to the uttermost reaches of his persona, nigh unto driving him out of his tree, making the veins of his temples stand out like the roads on the relief map he and Gilbert Krantz made for their geography project at Harding High—was damn well gonna get scratched!
—*Scott Beach*
San Francisco, Calif.

It was 3:24 of a snowy Saturday afternoon as Rick stared at the televised image of Marsha—she of the frowsy, split-ended, bleached blond hair, ghastly turquoise eye shadow, too much nose and not enough chin—cheering as her husband, Craig, caressed the enormous eagle-topped trophy, and wondered once again what kind of a woman would marry a professional bowler.
—*Charles Hamilton*
Baltimore, Md.

Being a nearsighted rapist was hard enough, even before the town was garrisoned by a Highland regiment.
—*Robert D. Norris, Jr.*
Tulsa, Okla.

"Raisins? Or flies?" thought Uncle Charlie to himself as he apprehensively picked the darkish lumps out of Aunt Tina's Custard Surprise and dropped them under the table for Laddieboy, who wagged his tail, ate them, and knew the answer, but didn't care, really. —*Bob Pollock*
Norwood, Mass.

It was rather dark outside—not the kind of dark that's so dark that you can't see anything at all, but only the kind of dark where you can just barely see things after you've waited to allow your eyes to adjust to the dark, which is called dark-adaptation, which you can do best if you get enough Vitamin A. —*Carol Deppe*
Corvallis, Oreg.

PLAIN
BROWN
WRAPPERS

The poor little wooden boy could only sit helplessly and watch while the old puppet maker, who was now his father and whom he had just told how a good fairy had turned him into a living boy without strings, worked on a new life-sized puppet of a young woman with really big hooters.

—*Michael E. Wear*
Calgary, Alberta

"Oh shit, it's the end of the world!" said Ralph, missing his last chance to demonstrate that he could differentiate between scatology and eschatology.   —*G. L. Goe*
Greenwood, Ind.

"You," said the Elder to the young minister, surprising him in a most unnatural act with the young—but mature—native girl, dashing completely the minister's hopes for continual international travel in the service of the Church, "are in no position to be a missionary!"   —*Stanford Lamb*
Philadelphia, Pa.

The last small tremors had left his disrobed body like rodents fleeing from a falling building and, lying on his back next to the snoozing Sister Monica Terriformo, Rev. Simon Sandstone looked up at the cracks in the plaster ceiling of the sleazy motel room and marveled at how the earth had truly moved for him, as if he were a cheap pre-fab home with no foundation and Sister Monica were the San Andreas Fault.

—*Jerry Miller*
Franklin, Ind.

"God, I'm confused!" Gladys ejaculated.

—*Jim Terr*
Santa Fe, N.Mex.

Surreptitiously between the yawning bays of Stendhal quartos and Gogol folios, Dewey and Marion boinked with studious regard for each other's pleasure zones—blithely oblivious to the union grievance they were committing—and when she smoothly ejaculated, "Dewey, oh Dewey do me!" he realized that they had started a new chapter together, one with a lot of sticky pages.

—*Christopher J. Hughes*
Toronto, Ontario

Edwina gazed up at the scaffold and recalled the strange but wonderful thing that happened to Mr. Quill just moments after the hanging.

—*James M. Terminiello*
Saddle Brook, N.J.

To some women, no doubt, he was a rutabaga casserole, jello lasagna, a Velveeta soufflé, but, to Melanie, Fred was a canapé among hors d'oeuvres, Akmak for her pâté, and gladly would she dip his baguette in her Camembert, his jellied eel in her Dijon—O, there was no indigestion about it: Fred was the sour cream for Melanie's baked potato.

—*William D. Mott-Smith*
Oakland, Calif.

Kim squealed with delight, her long blonde hair matted to her large, sumptuous, sunspeckled torso which glistened under the hot fluorescent lamp, as Tom, batting his thick, long, black, curly lashes at his only true love, reached down, down, down into his dark-blue designer Calvin Klein denim jeans and ever so slowly and gently coaxed out the only object that could hold Kim's attention and light her sexual desires, his wallet.

—*Elizabeth A. Kotas*
Bonny Rozell
Golden, Colo.

Transfixed in the wine cellar by the powerful shaft of light emanating from Sir Anthony Lordling's electric torch, young Timothy Cobbler protested, "I never laid a finger on your daughter, Sir Anthony, honest . . . unless you'd call *this* a finger!"

—*Jack Mackay*
Naperville, Ill.

"I'm outta here!" said Ralph, demonstrating that *coitus interruptus* was his specialty.

—*G. L. Goe*
Greenwood, Ind.

"You beast," she lustfully cajoled, failing to suppress a throaty giggle while reaching a languid arm back to adjust the imported silk pillows and simultaneously realizing he had just gnawed through her edible undies, the ones Rodney had given to her as a birthday present before, of course, she had adopted

this German shepherd whose paws were raking the sheets to shreds.
—John J. McLaughlin
Danbury, Conn.

Last night I once again found myself totally exhausted and gasping for breath after sex, and thought for the hundredth time, "Is it the passionate exuberance of our lovemaking which so tires me out, or is it having to blow up that goddamn inflatable doll?"
—Bob Pollock
Norwood, Mass.

"Stop it and start again," gasped Beverly breathlessly, stopping herself before she startled him by starting again, "but this time when you start it don't stop until at least I have started, and preferably, much preferably, don't stop until I have."
—David L. Hoof
Washington, D.C.

"I don't come cheap!" said the gigolo to the stout matron, who coyly fingered her expensive brooch.
—Wayne D. Worthey
Washington, D.C.

They had hired Felicia in spite of her speech impediment, and she went daily about her work singing, "Peelings, Wo Wo Wo, Peelings of love!" sweeping and cleaning and carefully lifting the used condoms into the trash container in the small Nevada brothel.
—Bill Reeves
Reno, Nev.

Down below us that first morning, thrusting up through the clammy, clotted-looking banks of smog, spermatically white and seminally dense, the towers of the office blocks rose like vast, angular phallic symbols; the plane's engines pulsed with a sonorous libido; the sky seemed as if spread, naked and pinioned, upon the wide coverlet of the universe; and inside, in the warm cabin, a perfume like the purest essence of salaciousness rose from between her breasts—themselves as perfect as propeller bosses—as they imprinted their exquisite datum upon the tingling skin of my ribcage when she turned toward me on the narrow seat we shared.

—*Norman H. C. Smith*
Sea Point, South Africa

"Oh no," thought Sheila as she awoke to find herself alone in the forest, the leaves sticking to the Vaseline and the familiar aching and soreness rising to an unbearable pitch, "not again!"

—*James E. Scoggan*
Houston, Tex.

The she-wolf, who had spent the night pacing the floor of the cave and biting her lips, greeted her finally returning mate with a snarled, "All right, who is the bitch?"

—*Sheila H. Benson*
Gallipolis Ferry, W.Va.

It wasn't that Jill didn't enjoy dating the strong and handsome Dr. Denny Kildare, it was just that his enemas were too damn strong.

—*W. A. Seaver*
Madison, S. Dak.

Twilight approached; the sun slipped between the flesh of the mountain peaks like a large gold suppository into the awaiting bowels of the earth; but Chet remained lost, knowing that, with the coming of night, he would be in deep shit.

—*Kathleen Tompkins*
La Honda, Calif.

Johnny had been caught; as he sat in a warm pool of guilt on the floor of his closet with a flashlight, his hands on his penis, and a copy of Dr. Westheimer's *The Fifth Appendage*, he melted from the heated intensity of his mother's stare-of-death and knew he was in for a whipping, but, due to his consummate understanding of chapter six, he was prepared to enjoy it.

—*John P. Doucet*
New Orleans, La.

OLD
DR. CRICKETT
CALLED FOR
NURSE JUNEBUG

Old Dr. Crickett called for Nurse Junebug to follow him
into Critterland, and they hurried after Annie Ant and Billy
Beetle, who had summoned them for help when Careless Cow
had stepped on Sally Snail and caused her pancreas to stick
out of her right ear.   —*Richard Weilburg*
                                                Houston, Tex.

"Wouldn't let me join in any reindeer games, eh?" thought
a bitter Rudolph, his red nose glowing angrily in the dense
fog, as he slipped from the bell-studded harness and watched
eight of his tormentors, a sleigh full of toys, and St. Nicholas,
too, smash into the mountain slope.

                                    —*Cora Williams Weisenberger*
                                       Richton Park, Ill.

It was money, and lots of it, that Timmy wanted, but he
could sell Lassie to the vivisectionists only once.

                                           —*Frank Oneil*
                                            Greenfield, Mass.

Once upon a time in a very charming land purpled by chipper butterflies and yellowed by a most pleasant sun, there lived a moral, dutiful and considerate young lad named Matthew (but I know you damned delinquents don't want to read about that sissy, so hide from your parents and I'll tell you about Grobioch—a vile, sadistic, bloodthirsty beast with a penchant for the warm intestines and still-pulsing hearts gouged from the hapless bodies of mean adults).   —*Shannon Bayless*
Piedmont, Okla.

He threw the peas on the floor and smeared his ca-ca on the wall, for that was his job; he was a baby.
—*Patrick Flanders*
Sunnyvale, Calif.

Once upon a time in a magical faraway land there lived a munchkin named Todd, who loved to while away his afternoons picking daisies, chasing butterflies, and making black puddings out of little children who happened to get caught in his trap lines.   —*Murray J. Munro*
Edmonton, Alberta

"Can you say 'webbed feet'?" asked Mr. Bodgers, unaware that he, a kindly media fixture for generations of Oakdale's children, had unwittingly broken, with his gentle question about pedal appendages, a carefully constructed conspiracy of silence that had reigned since the night, four years before, when bright flashes and roars of thunder had been heard from the western outskirts of the now-unused nuclear powerplant.
—*Charles Hamilton*
Baltimore, Md.

"Toadying to the Evil Queen might not be the best gig in the land," reflected the magic mirror, "but it sure beats working in a damn barber shop for minimum wage."

—*Richard Carter*
Hampton, Va.

Jack: act or move with easy alacrity, i.e. be agile, active, brisk, catlike, lively, sprightly, zippy, adroit, deft, dexterous, lithe, or supple; Jack: move, proceed, or act with great celerity, i.e. be fast, breakneck, expeditious, fleet, hasty, posthaste, raking, rapid, snappy, speedy, or swift (possibly apt, prompt, or punctual); Jack: please move suddenly through space by or as if by muscular action over the metallic, decoratively wrought object designed for the express purpose of holding tallow or wax molded around a wick, so that it may be burned to give light.

—*Larry Sherman*
Fremont, Calif.

Something told Dorothy she was not in Kansas anymore; maybe it was the color of the sky, maybe it was the air around her, maybe it was the sign on the side of the road that said, "Welcome to Missouri."

—*Kevin J. Day*
Richmond Hts., Mo.

Dorothy sobbed bitterly when her passionate love affair with the Tin Woodsman was cut short by a localized case of metal fatigue.

—*Dale Peter Cipperley*
San Jose, Calif.

Our heroine smoothed the skirt of her demurely long blue and white frock as she gazed into the mirror at her coal-black hair, reflected on the events which led her to the small cottage in the forest, and wondered whether the seven little old men with the funny names and strange habits would suspect that only a few weeks earlier she had been turning tricks out of a dingy motel room on the outskirts of Baltimore.

—*Don Roberts*
Orinda, Calif.

The virtuous Aribella, princess royal, beloved of all Lilitania, whose delicate, alabaster fingers rested tenderly as dove's wings upon the slender golden rail of the graceful balcony overlooking the palace courtyard in the fair and tranquil Lilitanian capital of Verlui, turned her eyes of palest green on the thronging, adoring crowd below and knew, with a certainty that alloyed heart and mind in the crucible-heat of understanding, that the entire, filthy lot of them were staring straight up her skirts.

—*Tom Wimbish*
Greensboro, N.C.

Teeny Tiny Timmy, the cutest little blue and yellow caterpillar with brown bristles and clean whiskers, always spent his time prattling and prattling about visiting London, driving his Mummy and Daddy and 1,238 brothers and sisters quite batty, when all of a sudden, Bobo the Big Bad Bird swooped down and picked up Teeny Tiny Timmy and took him to the city of his dreams where his remains can still be seen splattered on Lord Nelson's nose.

—*Marina True*
Berkeley, Calif.

Pretty Percy Pig and Jolly Molly Moo-Cow enjoyed watching the sunshiny green meadows and cheerful sparkling streams

of Pleasant Acres from Farmer Brown's new apple-red truck
on their way to the Rainbow Valley Meat Packing Company.
—*Eddie Lawhorn*
Huntsville, Ala.

As the five little pigs filled themselves up with beer, four
of them ran to the bathroom, leaving the fifth little pig to go
wee-wee-wee all the way home.   —*Michelle DeLong*
Mesa, Ariz.

THE
FIRST DAY
OF THE
IDITAROD

It was the third day of the Iditarod sled race, and a frigid
wind blew ice crystals into Preston's grizzled, windburned face
as he urged his dogs on: "Mush! Let's go, Jason, Jennifer,
Jeremy! Move it out, Chelsea, Brian! Come on, Buffy, Muffy,
Mush!"
                                                —*Michael J. Saxton*
                                                      Davis, Calif.

It was the eve of the yearly whale-slaughtering festival,
thought Mamook as her horny fingers relentlessly pushed the
whalebone needle through the sole of the mukluk; and suddenly, unaccountably, uncontrollably, she began to blubber.
                                                —*Debra Yoo Hessemer*
                                                      Chicago, Ill.

Nanook struggled out of the frigid arctic waters onto the ice
floe and realized, with the clarity only hindsight gives, that

putting the hibachi in his boat had been a mistake—he couldn't have his kayak and heat it, too.   —*Eddie Lawhorn*
Huntsville, Ala.

There was something about her that turned Kamuk on: perhaps it was her hair; perhaps it was her body; perhaps it was her husky voice (so husky it would pull a dog sled); no, it was definitely the way she clubbed seals.

—*Kyle B. Crocker*
Spokane, Wash.

A chill flowed down Bob's spine like an icy cataract and pooled in his bowels like a meltwater pond on a glacier as he suddenly realized that the tantalizingly familiar Second Secretary to the Chinese ambassador was in reality Innaugumpunct, the Eskimo shaman whose tribe's ancestral fishing waters had been totally destroyed by last year's oil spill, and that therefore the Pristine Waters Treaty, the final copy of which the President was even now signing, was likely to give the Chief Executive considerably more of a reputation in environmentalist circles than he had planned on.

—*W. Roy Wessel*
Boulder, Colo.

Were it not for the lack of a hard surface, the mud pygmies of New Guinea would have surely celebrated their good fortune when one hundred pairs of tap shoes destined for New Jersey were mistakenly sent to them.

—*Steven Snook*
East Syracuse, N.Y.

The only sounds in the dense rain forest were the drip, drip, drip of water falling on the leaves, the sort of schhhluup-thud, schhhluup-thud, schhhluup-thud of the poisoned darts as they formed a neat triangle in Bart's body, and the whispering of the two pygmies discussing the merits of Visa versus American Express. —*Leigh Robertson*
Dallas, Tex.

As PFC Robert Batson Gilderstern waded up to his neck through the slimy, putrid, disease- and snake-ridden swamp-water, weighted down with the twenty pounds of high explosives that his platoon so desperately needed, he never dreamed that he would die thirty years later from, of all things, an infection suffered as a result of biting his tongue while eating a piece of divinity at Monica's Christmas party.
—*Tom Hudson*
Huntsville, Ala.

As he heard the staccato tattoo of enemy bullets seeking the vitals of his Spitfire, he pushed the throttle of the Rolls-Royce Merlin engine to maximum, relishing the deep-throated roar while anticipating the thrill he was about to experience, nearly blacking out with the g-forces until he lined up his fighter and made a final reconnaissance pass over the East Upper Anglia Nudist Camp. —*Peter L. Manly*
Tempe, Ariz.

When I explained the facts of life to this primitive but voluptuous savage—*in vivo*—she stared up at me like a tree full of owls. —*W. R. C. Shedenhelm*
Ventura, Calif.

The glistening salty sweat slid past his hatband, silver rivulets trickling down between his furrowed brows, blurring the vision in his good eye and aggravating the injury the other had sustained that morning wrestling the rabid orangutan in the Mjari Pit of Death, slowed Vance's descent down the sheer granite face, and caused him to temporarily forget the grave peril in which poor Melissa had been placed by his unlucky cut of the cards, marvel at the sparkle of the mica fragments, reflecting the late afternoon African sun, and the wonderous texture of the massive stone face itself, and conclude that he must return here and hack a coffee table from this rock.

—*Kevin Lenagh*
Minneapolis, Minn.

As Kathleen reached the top of the sand dune, her hairdresser and stiletto heels miles behind, and looked across the vast expanse of the Mojave desert, she realized it looked just like the ocean, except, of course, there was no water.

—*Jennifer Dinkler*
Los Angeles, Calif.

Sweet as Aboud's lips were as he crushed her thigh urgently against the sand, Mandy's pride would not let her drown the duty of escape in the pomegranate juice of passion, never mind how welcome—and so her eye remained cunningly fixed upon the caravan of dromedaries, humping across the far-flung dunes.

—*William Spoehr*
Cuyahoga Falls, Ohio

The CIA was assigned to rescue the director of the FBI from his KGB abductors, which to Agent Junior Efrem's mind

was tantamount to hiring the Keystone Kops to rescue Curly from the Marx Brothers.   —*Mark Ditoro*
                                              Coraopolis, Pa.

As the Sandinista bodies piled up on the white tropical beach under the withering fire of her white-hot AK-46, Buffy Hearington knew two things: first, she was nowheres near Ft. Lauderdale and, second, that if she broke one more nail reloading, she would just scream   —*C. Steven Hager*
                                              Edmond, Okla.

He stood, a shell-shocked shell of a man in turquoise gabardine, reeling in the memories of the past nine hours—the hurled accusations from the dwarf Enrico, the ski lodge larder strewn with mangled pots and pans, the lurching flight through the marshes at dawn—and he marveled at the seasick sequence of events that had brought him here, a tangled figure in two-tone shoes, standing in silence on this craggy cliff at the edge of this really big desolate plain, a pair of cheap, sequined clown shoes in one hand and a battered muffin tin in the other.

—*Nancy Garner Ebert*
St. Paul, Minn.

Being stuck on a tropical island with only bunnies to eat (who multiplied after the shipwreck while we were surviving on saltwater Tang and fifty pounds of pickles), and in the company of a woman who, if any more frigid, would move three inches a year, is not a pleasant way to spend 33 years, 5 months, and 17 days.   —*Jeremy Rice*
                                              San Jose, Calif.

"Hands up, Infidels!" shouted the wild-eyed terrorist, holding aloft a hand grenade and interrupting a heretofore routine flight from Provo to Cheyenne, "or I'll scatter pieces of this plane all over the Great Basin, that region of the western United States between the Sierra Nevada and Wasatch Mountains which contains many isolated mountain ranges but has no drainage to either the Pacific Ocean or the Gulf of Mexico."
                                              —*David Willingham*
                                              Georgetown, Tenn.

After three torturous months at sea, I welcomed the sight of Bilge Keel Island the way a famished five-year-old welcomes the sight of a triple-scoop chocolate sundae; not artificial chocolate, mind you, but the honest-to-goodness rich, goopy kind that people swap their first-born sons for—the pride of Hershey, Pennsylvania; listen, pal, I'm talking about sugar, syrupy, sweet, succulent stuff that could bring tears to your eyes, even if you just saw a picture of it in a magazine, and it wouldn't even have to be in color.   —*Brian D. Smith*
                                              Indianapolis, Ind.

LYTTONY IV

> **Writing Tip #13: Characterization** In helping your readers visualize your characters, don't be afraid of drawing on familiar faces and personalities:
>
> "His friends agreed that he looked a lot like Bogart (the lean-faced Bogie of *Petrified Forest*), except that when he spoke it was with the unmistakable articulation of David Niven, and his physical gestures were those of Jerry Lewis in *The Nutty Professor*. Anyway, he was a real puzzle."

"Read my lips, damn you, read my lips!" Bossie pled inarticulately, as the queue moved forward toward the chute and certain death, but none of the attendants could understand her, much less read the tatooed legend on her great bovine lips: "National Science Foundation Experimental Bionic Cow; if found return to NSF Farm, Belton, Md., for reward.

—*Pete Saussy*
Columbia, S.C.

"Mr. President, you can't read my flips," observed Dr. Reggie Retina, optometrist, as he turned over yet another eye chart, "and you'll be in deep doo-doo if you don't take care of this vision thing." —*John L. Ashman*
Houston, Tex.

I knew, when I saw the sparkle in her eyes, the gentle curve of her nose, and the tiny sterling replica of the City and County

of Los Angeles dangling from her left ear, that this was to be
the mother of my children, the next president of the United
States, or just a good time.   *Paul Streeter*
                                                 Novato, Calif.

Not unlike the country in between Nigeria and the Sudan,
his name was Chad.   *—Jeff Kruse*
                                                Van Nuys, Calif.

As the big Ford station wagon spun crazily on the dark, rain-
slick road, Ward smacked his head on the steering wheel and
bit his pipe in half; June accidentally plunged her high heels
through the dashboard; Wally gripped an armrest and prayed
to God he would not die a virgin; and the Beaver's high-
pitched voice keened from the back seat, carrying with it the
ultimate horror of the Cleavers' misbegotten beach trip, "Gee,
Dad, you just ran over Lassie!"   *—R. L. Bryant*
                                                Columbia, S.C.

For some reason, Laura's first meeting with Lars, the son
of her fiancé's half-brother's cousin Emma's Uncle from Upp-
sala, was not memorable.   *—Jean B. Brownell*
                                                Portland, Oreg.

The tardy bell, which causes a spasm in the shoulders of
the Language Arts teacher in room 209 as she stares at the
last tree remaining on the school hillside, who today seems to
have come in costume—pinstripe skirt, ramie blouse and al-
ligator shoes which belie her more familiar Birkenstock san-
dals, pointed-hemmed crepe skirt and rag wool sweater and
hints of the long-past disco days of multizippered slit skirt,
dark roots and bangles, and who sips her espresso from a brown

paper cup and watches animated fourteen-year-olds to their chairs while she ponders whether to follow the usual route to her family home at Wing Point or turn left on 305 and send a postcard from the panda exhibit of the San Diego Zoo (lately, she found herself thinking about endangered animals), thereby causing a flurry of rumors that would inspire letters to the editor by authors who create scenarios to explain her disappearance written, ironically enough, in the run-on sentence style she had devoted her life to suppressing, rang.

> —*Dana Marrs*
> *Bainbridge Island, Wash.*

Harold choked on his potato salad even though it was mashed potato salad that his wife always made, and not the diced potato salad that his mother used to make, but recovered in time to cry out, "Harriet, why do you always have to bring that book which you know I don't like to be read to out of up for?"

> —*Lloyd P. Elliott*
> *Topeka, Kans.*

What with the cold night air and the rain pouring down, it was somewhat comforting to have a roof over my head and four walls around me; now if only the walls had been joined together and the roof repositioned horizontally so as to keep the rain off, I would have been in great shape.

> —*Craig Oakley*
> *Berkeley, Calif.*

Armed with some helpful hints from Home Economics 213 ("Creative Fabrics"), Gladys discovered that you could indeed make a silk purse out of a sow's ear—and thus was born Hog

Togs, the company which was soon to bring her fame, fortune, and romance with a clinical psychologist.

—Karen C. Huber
Colorado Springs, Colo.

If'n there was one thang that Alamo know'd, it was that he wanted to be all over Miss Amy like a oil slick on a sea otter—shucks—he'd commenced ta seein' her purdy face everywhere, even now in those tiny sun-dappled bubbles poppin' and fizzin' at his feet as he slowly zipped his britches an hobbled outta the holler.

—Glenn Bering
Ann Arbor, Mich.

What joy to encounter the aspect of the sun coming up over the mountains, when the tallest thing I had ever seen was the Dairy Queen sign at Crupper's Corner that they put up last year right before the tornado blew it right through Brantley's Drug Store and they lost Aunt Josie's prescription.

—Lucile Addington
Dallas, Tex.

Bombay, Bombay, Bombay, Bombay! thought Beatrice as the sluggish Hooglie River slid slowly astern of the tramp steamer; Bombay—the city and the gin . . . Oh I do love you both!

—Foster Bam
Greenwich, Conn.

IN
DUBIOUS
TASTE

"There is no free will," said the old sage, "for you may not choose your parents nor the hour of your birth, neither may you select the time and manner of your death, nor may you have any voice in what passes in between, although if you can afford a good plastic surgeon, you might be able to pick your own nose."
—*Brian Holmes*
San Jose, Calif.

The partially clouded moon rose like a half-eaten marshmallow over a weenie-roasted horizon, making the field of dead Girl Scouts look even more grim and foreboding, in spite of the unusual crispness of the air.
—*Margaret Baker*
Philadelphia, Pa.

His heart fluttering, he felt the familiar intoxicating sense of power verging on awe as strains of Beethoven's "Ode to Joy" drifted into his consciousness, rising in its stirring crescendo, confirming to the core of his being the absolute art of what he was about to do, and with an electrifying thrill shud-

dering through his body, Dr. Forquin thrust the liposuction tube deftly and deeply into Mrs. Mulch's bulbous left buttock.
—*Eva M. Koepsell*
Sanborn, N.Y.

Running out of the bathroom, the earthquake hit with devastating alacrity as Muffie moaned maniacally, "As God is my witness, I'll never need Milk of Magnesia again."
—*C. T. Brooke*
Pleasant Hill, Calif.

Diarrhea runs in my family.
—*Eddie Lawhorn*
Huntsville, Ala.

from *The Old Man and the Seat:*
He was an old man who sat alone in an outhouse near the stream and it had been three days since he had taken a crap.
—*Peter P. Kettell*
No. Kingstown, R.I.

No one seemed to know the real name of the gnarled old man with the merry twinkle in his one good eye, but all the boys and girls in the neighborhood called him "Mr. Nickels" because, if you said the magic words "Mr. Nickels's nose knows nickels," he'd oblige you by blowing his nose into a bright red and yellow hanky, then, with a conspiratorial wink, which of course momentarily blinded him, he'd let you open the hanky and, if you were lucky, you'd find a bright, shiny new nickel as often as not.
—*Marty Fleck*
Houston, Tex.

Sitting patiently at my feet, gazing adoringly into my face, my faithful weimaraner of twelve years, Hans, bright as he was, could not begin to comprehend the utter dejection I felt at being dumped by that arrogant shoe salesman who, just because he wore a three-piece suit, tried to pass himself off as a successful business executive at fancy restaurants, and who winked and flirted with every female under forty (and in my company!); and reaching for another tissue I wondered again why dogs don't have boogers.   —*Connie Fox*
                                                Carbonado, Wash.

Moira's delicate, off-white breasts were not unlike the perfectly formed mounds of buttery, wholesome mashed potatoes she daintily proffered to each ravenous, well-scrubbed ragamuffin; and she took a fierce Irish pride in the creamy, lumpless texture of both.   —*Marilyn D. Rauch*
                                                Worthington, Ohio

from *To Mock a Killing Bird:*
As Freddie the falcon flew home with his belly empty again he heard the other falcons taunt him with "You couldn't catch a mouse if it was blind!" and "Ha, you call yourself a raptor!" and worst of all, "Put some nail polish on your talons, sissy boy!"   —*Michele Fagin*
                                                Hartford, Vt.

Auntie Epiglotta was quite peeved with me when I called the nurse in the Pneumonia Ward a phlegm fatale, saying she

just could not swallow that type of humor, she just could not hack it, it choked her up and made her so mad she could spit.
—*John McKinstry*
Big Sur, Calif.

Bob, the plumber's helper, grunting and panting and grinding his teeth, drove hard in and out of the slimy, wet hole, beating against the rubbery obstruction, giving a little twist at the end of each stroke, while Mrs. McGillicuddy, her forehead damp, her hair in disarray, moaned and bit her lip, saying, "Why does it always clog just before my cotillion?"
—*Dan Mason*
Mountain View, Wyo.

"So this," mused Philip as he watched Zen Master Steve repeatedly bend the severed piece of limb in half, causing the bones to produce a faint but audible crunching noise, "is the sound of one hand clapping."
—*Murray J. Munro*
Edmonton, Alberta

With his powerful, slow strides, Jacques showed off his rakish good looks—his huge, battle-scarred head and his torn ear—but it wasn't until he indolently sprayed on the Swedish Empire sofa that Fluffy knew him to be the mate of her own heart.
—*Marina True*
Berkeley, Calif.

No matter what you called her—strumpet, doxy, drab, bag, lady of the night, concubine, whore, harlot, hussy, hooker, tart, trollop, pickup, wench, minx, meretrix, or demimondaine—you had to admit, Sadie never missed a trick.
—*Reed Bowman*
Albany, Calif.

"E.T.,
GO HOME!"

Eliot glared at the little creature, now skewered ten feet up the road on the broken branch of a pine tree, which, by sitting in the front basket of his until recently undamaged bike, had blocked his vision of Mrs. Tittleworthy's now dented station wagon, and, rubbing his scraped knee, hissed, "E.T., go home!"
—*Matthew R. Kratter*
Bellevue, Wash.

Sir Herzog, Duke of the small area of open land between Schwartzenwald Forest and the Weisfluss River, also known as Graufeld, raised his sword Schwert, the finest and final work in steel by that greatest of swordsmiths, Grobschmied, and brought it down on the nape of the neck of the great dragon Drache, the largest and most ferocious and fearsome of his kind ever seen in Winzigdorf, so hard and at just the right angle that it passed through and struck sparks from the marble floor, produced by fantastic heat and incomprehensible pressure acting on buried limestone over millions of years.
—*Gabe Kramer*
Colorado Springs, Colo.

Gnawing her cuticles into shredded coconut, Zelda wondered how she could defuse the potential interplanetary in-

cident she had created by accidentally making tea out of the
Ambassador from Planeria.   —*Marcia Bednarcyk*
                                                   Palo Alto, Calif.

   Nigia, Conan's illegitimate half-sister and mother of two,
swung her graphite fishing rod that doubled as a broadsword
in a dizzying arc, severing the first head, and, without losing
momentum, spun and buried the gleaming blade into the
second head of the giant two-headed Swamp Slug, somer-
saulted over the carcass using the beautifully jeweled hilt that
got accidentally chipped last summer hamstringing a cyclops,
and finished the wash the way any forty-nine-year-old Black
Amazon Swordswoman would.   —*Juanita Lewison-Snyder*
                                   Coos Bay, Oreg.

   Sulu had reservations about Atari Corporation's refit of the
Enterprise every time he had to stick another quarter into the
navigation console.   —*Dale Peter Cipperley*
                                            San Jose, Calif.

   They fell from the vastness of the azure sky, a plethora
of twinkling and blinking scarlet and yellow beacons on
aircraft no bigger than a five-grain aspirin tablet, setting
down their tiny feet upon the still-green unripened ears in
Daphne Magillicutty's cornfield, making it appear as
though Christmas had arrived six months too early—or too
late.

                                           —*Pamela Cantrell*
                                            Las Vegas, Nev.

Horrid green aliens from planet Grrr now rule my city with their ghastly legions, whereas before the place was predominately white.   —*Jeff Kruse*
                                                                                    Van Nuys, Calif.

Her taut young Earth bosom heaving and her skin flushed with passion, Jessica struggled vigorously (if only for form's sake) with the alien creature as it undressed her with its eyes (which grew at the end of long prehensile stalks and were quite adroit with snaps and fasteners), reflecting that no matter what her mother thought, Xytrons sure beat the geeks she dated back in Kansas.   —*Richard Carter*
                                                                                    Hampton, Va.

Suddenly the tiny advanced civilization on Aktak was vaporized as that planet's red sun burst into a supernova, destroying eons of knowledge and enlightenment, while 30,000 light-years away Elizabeth turned on "General Hospital" and began making pigs from her blue and green Play-Doh.
                                                                                    —*Doug Robinson*
                                                                                    Fayetteville, Ga.

Looking back at the hundred-week Ratings War, in which the cutthroat competition between the major TV networks escalated into actual attacks at one another's jugulars, few would deny that the controversial event which sparked this confrontation was the live voodoo ceremony, reviving Walt Disney from his casket in Disneyland, climaxed by Mickey Mouse as the Sorcerer's Apprentice, turning the entire tribe

of Smurfs into blue magic mushrooms and roasting them over
a spit.   —*Lawrence Wong*
                                         San Francisco, Calif.

Samuel snickered while tearing the cellophane from his
completely lifelike fully automatic electric love android, little
realizing how its poor review in *Consumer Reports* would affect
his sex life until an exciting event involving frayed insulation
and a leaky waterbed.   —*Dale Peter Cipperley*
                                         San Jose, Calif.

The time tunnel was closing rapidly as Betsy Mae frantically
dragged her toaster through the opening; morning in the
twenty-third century would be a nightmare without Pop Tarts.
                                         —*Carol Babst*
                                         San Jose, Calif.

(with apologies to Douglas Adams)
   Far out in the backwaters of the unfashionable end of the
Western Spiral arm of the Galaxy lies a small unregarded yellow sun, and orbiting this at a distance of roughly eight
hundred ninety-nine million ten thousand miles is the flash-
frozen body of Farley Wilsputz, Jr., and boy is there an interesting story of how he came to be a component of Saturn's
ring system.

                                         —*Richard Garrett*
                                         Pittsburgh, Pa.

Being turned into a cockroach was a shock of epic proportions, but at least Twinkies still tasted the same.

—*Jeremy Rice*
San Jose, Calif.

"Great heavens, Jeremy!" exclaimed Dr. Martinson to his laboratory assistant as they cowered side by side under a Formica-topped table, peering out surreptitiously at the pulsating green fronds that oozed menacingly from the bubbling network of test tubes precariously suspended over a Bunsen burner, "do you think it will go well with Hollandaise sauce?"

—*Janet M. Goldstein*
Rose Valley, Pa.

"Into the air lock!" Captain Barney ordered as Khodan death rays lanced through the skin of our ship, causing a catastrophic decompression that forced Captain Barney to balloon like . . . well, like a balloon, until his exploding body shredded his suit into a thousand pieces, much like the confetti found at a postwar victory party—a celebration I intuitively knew we would probably not attend.

—*Phil C. Fry*
Toledo, Ohio

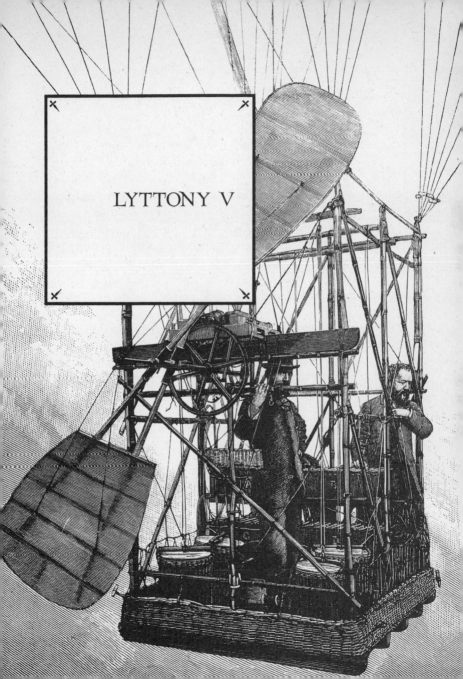

LYTTONY V

Writing Tip #16: Openings Literary professionals suggest that a novel start right away with some kind of action. One great idea we like is to have the main character in an airplane circling an airport to land. This situation gives you plenty of time to have the person soul-search, review the past, make plans, catch a nap, whatever. If the process becomes lengthy, give the plane lots of fuel and put it into a holding pattern. Such traffic jams are becoming increasingly common-place at today's airports. And if you find yourself losing interest in the character and decide you want to write your novel about someone else, you can easily rid yourself of your creation in a way calculated to delight your readers and offend the FAA.

The lustful Empress of China, wishing to satisfy her lascivious desires with several new love slaves, compelled the captured Mongol army to march in the nude for hours beneath the harsh Hunan sun before she finally announced her choice: one from column A and two from column B.

—*Brian W. Holmes*
San Jose, Calif.

"What is this sad world but an infinitesimal dust bunny in the unimaginably vast broom closet that we call the universe?" I asked, before being told to shut up. —*Jeff Kruse*
Van Nuys, Calif.

It was at moments like this, with the snow drifting gently past the window on a crisp winter night as he sat in front of the crackling fire holding her hand and gazing into her eyes, that he often wondered what had become of the rest of her.

—*Peter Tilley*
Englewood, Colo.

"Daughter," he said, "I am an old man now, but I have seen the bulls run at Pamplona, and I have sailed the Atlantic alone, and I have cracked up a plane in the jungle of Africa; however, I have yet to see the American public develop a sufficient vocabulary so that I will not feel impelled to write in my annoyingly simplistic style."   —*Claire Ball*
Kailua, Hawaii

Muffie swallowed hard as she added a few more drops of arsenic to the pumpkin bisque, the last pumpkin bisque that Kevin, false Kevin, would ever taste, just as the door chime went "Muff-ie!"   —*Scott Beach*
San Francisco, Calif.

from *A Warm Database:*
Bill would always remember the day he first met Jane; it would be forever imaged in his brain like a color video, with a complete sensory database included at no extra charge.

—*David Kenway*
Juneau, Alaska

Lilly Meredith Trebeck pulled her black support pantyhose tight up against her crotch, squatting once to adjust the seat portion, released the elastic waistband from her manicured fingers with a resounding snap, and slipped into a tastefully

suggestive Italian silk dress and three-inch heels with the re-
solve of a woman who damn well intended to control what
would happen on this day of all days.　　 —*S. L. Rizk*
Pasadena, Calif.

I don't like horses—their faces are too long—and this one
didn't like me, as I could tell when it turned too short and
hooked the buggy wheel around the gatepost and I didn't
know what to do—there's not any steering wheel, you know—
and made that stupid noise while it jerked and stood on its
hind legs while I was trying to see the damage to my dress
and pantyhose from landing in some mud and thinking what
an entrance I'd make up at the big house.

—*Lucile R. Addington*
Dallas, Tex.

The first indication I had that things were not quite as they
should be in my host's household was when I noticed that his
butler dragged his foot behind him . . . on a rope.

—*Richard W. O'Bryan*
Perrysburg, Ohio

The raucous, ecstatic laughter of little Nigel, the evil one,
rent the air as the acrid odor of singeing dog hair drifted downstairs, triggering the smoke alarm, and the spaghetti, scorching
in its pot, boiled over, oozing down the front of the stove and
across the floor to where tiny, sweet Harold stood happily
pushing silverware down the disposal when the loutish master
of the house, aflame with desire, crept up behind the nubile
young French girl, crushing her in his arms, his hoary breath

hot upon her breasts, as she suddenly sensed that the life of an *au pair* might not be exactly as described in the brochure.

—*Barbara Cleaver Kroll*
Kennett Square, Pa.

Irving R. Fachtfeinder, head reference librarian, could never let any question go unanswered, and while he was generally considered a colossal bore, his overstuffed cranium rested easy each night with the comforting knowledge that he, and he alone, knew where all the flowers had gone, how things were in Glocca Morra, and who put the overalls in Mrs. Murphy's chowder.

—*Pamela Wylder*
Bloomington, Ind.

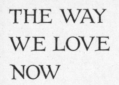

THE WAY
WE LOVE
NOW

Jake liked his women the way he liked his kiwi fruit: sweet yet tart, firm-fleshed yet yielding to the touch, and covered with short brown fuzzy hair. —*Gretchen Schmidt*
Coral Gables, Fla.

As Roselyn downed her fifth margarita, she thought to herself that men were not unlike snowmen: they are easily made, they have only white fluffy stuff between their ears, they get squishy when they sit around too long, and they disappear when things get hot. —*Kathy Mueller*
Franklin, Ind.

Penny couldn't remember her name and, what was worse, after she regained consciousness she couldn't remember whether or not she had a boyfriend, and if she did she didn't know who or where he was or whether he'd tested positive.
—*Lorrie Evelyn Furrer*
Columbia, Mo.

Savoring her tryst with the dashing Dexter Bosox, Sheila stroked Milhous, her top maze-running rat, quite ignorant that Dexter and the sniveling rodent shared a like appreciation for her attentions—and all when she thought they had nothing in common but perfect hair.   —*Deane Morrison*
                                   Minneapolis, Minn.

Primrose knew instinctively—with the unknowing knowing common to all of her sex—the minute she met Lord Basin-stroke's eyes that he was the only man she could or would ever love, at least until they got a houseboy.

                                   —*Kimberly Colley*
                                   Union, Ky.

Elizabeth pensively bit her lip with such force that it began to bleed profusely and panicked as she realized that one of her violet-colored contacts was perched precariously on the tip of Geoffrey's aristocratic nose, and desperately wondered if he had noticed her exposed pink iris and come to the realization that she was not of Jamaican descent (as she had led him to believe) but really an albino from Chicago wearing a dark wig and five gallons of Bain de Soleil.

                                   —*Shannon Walker*
                                   Redwood City, Calif.

Her mouth said, "No! no! no!" but every other inch of her throbbing glistening body said, "Yes! yes! yes!" except for her pancreas, which didn't care much either way.

                                   —*Jacob Solomon Weinstein*
                                   Washington, D.C.

"I'm only kidding!" said Anthony as he twisted Sarah's long hair around his brawny hand and pushed her protesting body over the railing, to dangle helplessly over the formal garden below, with its yew trees clipped into the shapes of roosters.

—*Bea Liu*
Minneapolis, Minn.

His hot breath seared her neck and interrupted her careful listing of how many full roses as opposed to how many half roses were present on the antique wallpaper in this upstairs bedroom of the old house that let the swirling wind whisper through the cracks in the windows. —*Colleen Marron*
Fremont, Calif.

The garden was in full bloom by late May, and Norman noted with a certain pride that the hyacinths were particularly lush directly over the spot where Marsha had cursed him one final time through a mouthful of dirt. —*Tom Wimbish*
Greensboro, N.C.

Madrid is a fascinating city except I couldn't speak Spanish so I can't tell you a lot about that summer when I met Ricardo except I'm 5′4″ and he came up to my bellybutton.

—*June Obrochta*
Pittsburgh, Calif.

Vance had showered Marie with kisses, leaving her vibrant with desire, splendidly joyous, and covered with those little flies that seem to be attracted to dried saliva.

—*Larry Sherman*
Fremont, Calif.

She raised the barrel of her Browning 20-gauge and aimed for Daniel's lower chakras.
                                                —*Shannon Bayless*
                                                Piedmont, Okla.

Some men called her Sue because they fought long and hard over her; other men called her Rose because they felt either great joy or great pain when holding her tight; still others called her Black Maria because they landed in jail after messing around with her; so I called her Friday because I looked forward to seeing her after a long week.
                                                —*Lawrence Wong*
                                                San Francisco, Calif.

The reflection of the moon poured across the water like spilled milk across a black velvet painting of Elvis recently acquired in Tijuana and caused the sky above to luminesce steely gray like radioactive zombie skin and light the uncurtained bedroom where Cynthia slept, unaware that Lyle crouched at the side of her massive four-poster plotting how he would have his way with her without disturbing her REM pattern.
                                                —*Dean M. Christianson*
                                                Pacifica, Calif.

Samantha's bosom roiled like piglets in a poke as Armand's hands touched her shoulders, burning her like ground-beef patties on a searing-hot grill, and she melted to him like Velveeta to toasted French bread, their passion boiling up like oil in the fry cooker of desire; and as he clicked off her microphone and drew her down to the duckboards, her paper cap falling off of her richly shining auburn hair, she knew she

would finally learn the utmost secrets of drive-thru burger
stand love.   —*George V. Vinson*
                                                        Turlock, Calif.

Linda, single into her early thirties, dreaded calling her
married sister because she always had to suffer through a discussion about her two-year-old nephew and six-month-old
niece, a discussion focused almost entirely on urination and
defecation including, but not limited to, size, consistency,
color, frequency, and medication, but her sister was the only
one with whom she could talk frankly about boyfriends and
sex including, but not limited to, size, consistency, color,
frequency, and medication.   —*Leonard Tobias*
                                                        Sunnyvale, Calif.

L'amour et la vie, oh pooh.   —*Rosina Yue*
                                                        Tesuque, N.Mex.

As was his custom, Walter parked the DeSoto on the front
lawn, exited the vehicle, sidestepped a pile the neighbor's
cockapoo, Murphy, had left for him, kicked an empty Stroh's
can into the dying junipers, and threw open the sagging screen
door, bellowing, "Hey, Tramp, I'm home!" as he always did—
but only silence and the odor of the cat's litter box greeted
him, for Gretchen was on the Greyhound bound for Oxnard
and deliverance.   —*Terrence Carroll*
                                                        San Jose, Calif.

MORE
VILE
PUNS

As Wilbur, long obsessed though unfamiliar with Pointilism, escorted his wife, Katy, into the Modern wing of the local art museum, he exclaimed jubilantly, "Kay, Seurat! Seurat!" to which she replied yawningly, "Whatever, Wilby, Wilby."
                    —*Matthew Kaslow*
                    Brooklyn, N.Y.

Because the adulterous stamp collector had a rotten memory, she was forever asking her paramour, "Have I told you, Phil, lately that I love you?"   —*Rev. William F. Charles*
                    Minneapolis, Minn.

"Serf's up!" the unwashed crowd roared as the sheriff raised Lud the Miller's body on a pole, demonstrating the medieval genius for spontaneous humor at its best.
                    —*David Willingham*
                    Georgetown, Tenn.

As she gazed out on her vast, inherited farmland, which was now overrun by an extraordinarily plentiful crop of potatoes, farmer Jones thought ruefully to herself, "I'm going to have to get some of these tubers tied."   —*Douglas Edelson*
                    East Meadow, N.Y.

Lady Jessica could appreciate sentimental value as well as the next person, but she really felt deep down that old family retainers were not the best solution for her overbite.
—*Lucy West*
Grand Prairie, Tex.

In the fertile valley of the Euphrates, shining their shoes and figuring out their income tax, the tribe of Jacob waxed and multiplied.
—*Carl Pavel*
Chicago, Ill.

Father O'Flaherty pulled his spindle chair closer to the rectory table, eyed his usual evening repast of purloined sacramental wine, Stilton, and Brie displayed before him, and murmured contentedly, "What a friend we have in cheeses!"
—*Jim Ratzenberger*
Vienna, Va.

Algernon lay curbside and face downward in the wretched rain, retching toward the drainage, which, together with his tortured intestines, made gutteral sounds.
—*Charles T. Zlatkovich*
Austin, Tex.

The old man looked at his devastated flock and sighed as he parceled out the few remaining sheep to his sons, "Jake can have the ram and Al can have the yearlings," then petting his favorite as she nuzzled him said, "and this ewe's for Bud."
—*Peter L. Manly*
Tempe, Ariz.

Ed, deathgrip-like, clutched the decayed, gas-bloated calf carcass to his soiled leisure suit and pleaded shrilly to the unamused stewardess, "but the rules say it's okay to take along carrion luggage!"
                        —*Jaan Pesti*
                        Wilmington, Del.

Just before ample Aunt Penny expired she made two final requests: to join the church, and be cremated, for as she so eloquently put it, "A Penny saved is a Penny urned."
                        —*Robert L. Schlosser*
                        Seattle, Wash.

The Cannes crowd booed at the screening of my feature-length film about Dobermans, but they absolutely adored my boxer shorts.
                        —*June T. Munger*
                        Boulder, Colo.

Up ahead, at the edge of the badlands, the trail split three ways, so Rex Savage, famous as the fastest gun west of Tucumcari, let his tired pony shuffle through the dust while he grappled with his options—would it be the West Trail, leading to California and Sue (the only woman he had ever really loved, who had promised to be waiting if he ever hung up his ivory-handled .44's), or the East Trail, to his dream of a degree from Yale Law School, or perhaps the North Trail, where his old Civil War buddy President Grant had promised to appoint him Indian agent for the entire Dakota Territory; "So which is it going to be," Rex pondered: "Sue, sue, or Sioux?"
                        —*R. F. Perkins*
                        Milwaukee, Wis.

The fifth ice age first manifested itself in Scotland, as if God wanted his Scotch on the rocks. —*Richard Patching*
Calgary, Alberta

This will be a marketing concept to rival mashed, preformed potato chips in a can, mused Merlin McDivot, Magician to the Masses, as he recalled his pride in perfecting the technique of preserving evil spells in thin metal packages; his dismay in discovering that the spells tended to go bad while his customers worked up their nerve to use what they had bought; and his joy in realizing that the problem could be overcome by replacing the package at a fraction of the cost of recharging the spell, so that the charms and cantrips could be stored indefinitely; the sign proclaiming his revolutionary method was, even now, being hung in his modest shop window— CURSES FOILED AGAIN. —*Charles Hamilton*
Baltimore, Md.

Theiu Hands (one of the few female entomologists from Vietnam and now married to an English clockmaker employed at the Royal Observatory in Greenwich) today submitted her first professional paper to "Tick-Talk: The Journal for the Study of the Ixodidae Family of Arachnids," figuring that both time and mite were right. —*Jay P. Maille*
Union City, Calif.

Once a month, when the moon is full, Reverend Jim Bleaker and his lovely wife, Teddi, invite members of the church to the parsonage for an evening of hymn singing, followed by

cookies, tea, and a frenzied orgy on the lawn outside, making sure, of course, to take all the usual precautions for safe sects.
—*Brian W. Holmes*
San Jose, Calif.

from *America, Eats to West*:

On their annual summer eating tour of the U.S., veteran overeaters Mike and Monica Swallow were thrilled with the street vendors in Philadelphia (which, they happily noted, allowed them to stuff their faces and cover ground at the same time), and so they waddled from street corner to street corner until Mike (ever the joker) walked backward across Market Street with a hot dog stuck in each ear (commenting that a frank with the works sure sounded good) and thus didn't hear Monica's anguished cry which was garbled by a hot pretzel (with mustard) but was reported by horrified bystanders to be, "Watch out for the hoagie car, Michael!" —*Pamela Wylder*
Bloomington, Ill.

"RUMBLING, SCHMUMBLING!" RETORTED BULONIUS

Writing Tip #18   Some fledgling writers have trouble showing that time has passed. One unobtrusive way to indicate the passage of time is to use some object:

"He looked up at the wall clock. Earlier it had said 1:30; now it said 5:15."

"Rumbling, Schmumbling!" retorted Bulonius to his wife's alarm at the sounds coming from Mt. Vesuvius, "that stupid volcano always makes noise—and besides, our insurance agent at Pompeii Mutual says that if it does erupt we'll be covered."
—*John L. Ashman*
Houston, Tex.

Reining in his battle steed before the imperial tent, mighty Caesar brandished his mace and chain at the limp form of the Celtic female draped across his saddle and triumphantly proclaimed to his cheering legions, "I came. I saw. I conked her!"—little realizing that he had coined a phrase destined to ring down through the millennia and survive the empire itself.
—*Marty Fleck*
Houston, Tex.

Pepin smiled with content as he checked his daily planner: wenching till noon, bear-baiting at 3:00, and vassal-flogging

right on up to evening prayers; life at the top sure was good
in the year 1306.
                                                —*G. L. Goe*
                                                Greenwood, Ind.

"Well, Maman always said that I would lose my head if it
weren't attached to me!" thought Desmoulins as the guillotine
blade whizzed past his ears, and now that it wasn't, he had—
thus getting a head start on the French Revolution.
                                                —*Cheryl Solimini*
                                                Martin Farawell
                                                Montclair, N.J.

The messenger from London rode like the very wind over
the purple moor, his spurs blood-red and his steed striking
sparks from the ribbon-of-moonlight road, for he literally car-
ried in his hands the life of his brother, who was now within
an ace of the gallows; of course he also bore the inevitable
concurrent concomitant to a Royal Pardon: orders revoking the
commission of whoever it was who would be played by George
Sanders.
                                                —*Robert D. Norris*
                                                Tulsa, Okla.

The quartermaster-general quickly scribbled a message and
gave it to his captain, saying, "Convey this to Lord Cardigan
immediately—he should get a charge out of it."
                                                —*Tony Kahman*
                                                Winslow, Ark.

Paul von Hindenburg, only one month old and wrapped in
a blue blanket, rested peacefully in his cradle, oblivious to

the tragedy that would one day befall a dirigible to be named
after him.   —*Kenneth Leffler*
                                                       Falls Church, Va.

It was a dark and swarmy night in somnolent prewar Hawaii
as Elinore, the admiral's lovely raven-tressed daughter, and
Lieutenant Rodney wrestled in the patio's tentative seclusion
with the depth of their passion on the knobby wrought-iron
bench, skin glistening golden with slick sweat and true love's
musky scent, in the shafting smoky sulfurous light of the
citronella's torches, oblivious to the batlike shadows cast over
them by Hirohito's numberless Zeros droning tumescently
overhead toward Pearl, when, sighing petulantly at desire's
crest, she huskily asked of him, "Rodney, the bugs are bad
tonight; where's the Raid?"   —*Jim Hirshfeld*
                                                       Detroit, Mich.

The column of cavalry halted at Dirty Butter Creek while
our scout, "Rhode Island Mort" MacGroombaum, rode forward to palaver in sign language with the solitary Comanche
atop Conger Eel Butte; he returned to report, "Waal, Loo-
tenant, that thar jasper is either the head cheese of all these
here Injuns and means to lift our hair, *or* he's a deaf-mute
piano-tuner from Turkey come west to sell aluminum siding
to the Tri-Delt house at Baylor; it jest depends on which sign
lingo he's using."   —*Robert D. Norris, Jr.*
                                                       Tulsa, Okla.

Adam awoke on the morning of the Sabbath, wincing at the
pain in his side and toying with the idea of putting in a few

hours' work; after all, he had a lot of animals yet to name and the creature Eve was no help at all.

—Aurlie Jaye Stewart
Redondo Beach, Calif.

"If you think I'm going to get on board with all of those animals," said Noah's wife testily, "you don't have all of your oars in the water!"   *—John L. Ashman*
Houston, Tex.

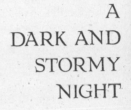

A
DARK AND
STORMY
NIGHT

"It was a dark and stormy night; the rain fell in torrents—except at occasional intervals, when it was checked by a violent gust of wind which swept up the streets (for it is in London that our scene lies), rattling along the housetops and fiercely agitating the scanty flame of the lamps that struggled against the darkness."
—opening sentence of *Paul Clifford* (1830)

King Louis, oblivious to the clear, star-studded evening beyond the castle walls, regally tapped the flat of his jeweled sword on the frail shoulders of the virginal maiden and pronounced stormily, "I dub thee, Jeanne d'Arc, knight."
—*H. Winton Ellingsworth*
Tulsa, Okla.

Jacques LeFleur, descendant of Jeanne d'Arc and the world's foremost carver of chessmen, stared intently at the face of his latest creation, agonizing whether to put it up for sale, thereby having to part with his new offspring, or, as he did with the large majority of his creations, to hold on to it in his already overpopulated attic, when he finally received the answer from the hollowed, anguished eyes: It was a d'Arc kin store-me knight.
—*Leonard Tobias*
Sunnyvale, Calif.

Sir Bulwer cringed, as much as the shackles allowed, as the royal torturer began his daily litany of verbal abuse—reminding the broken prisoner of his capture in an ill-lit mercantile, by smirking, "It was a darkened store, me knight!"

—*Eddie Lawhorn*
Huntsville, Ala.

It was a dark and stormy Knight who propelled the chair that skittered across the arena after the referee's whistle had frustrated him—the Hoosier Horatio, the nemesis of basketball officials (locally and nationwide), the man-for-man defender of inalienable rights (and lefts, too), the barking Bobby, the coach with the salt-and-pepper hair and personality.

—*Art Poulin*
Concord, Calif.

Once upon a time, a dark knight, probably from Ethiopia, where some knights are darker than others, went out on a dark night, probably in Alaska, where some nights are darker than others, and this knight simply disappeared into the dark night, so the king issued an edict stating: "Dark knights go out on light nights and light knights go out on dark nights and no one goes anywhere if it is stormy!"

—*Frankye D. Thompson*
Astoria, Oreg.

It was a dark and stormy night, but Lester West Chester, U.S. Patent Examiner, slept undisturbed in his bed, said bed comprising in combination a mattress, a box spring, a headboard, and support means, said support means comprising at least four metallic members, and wheel and axle means,

wherein said wheel and axle means are attached perpendicularly to the plane of said metallic members, and wherein further one end of said support means is adapted for supporting said headboard means. —*Kenneth Leffler*
Falls Church, Va.

It was that time of the circadian rhythm when the solar globe was away over the antipodean regions and should have been leaving the stage of the heavens to her selenian consort, except that tonight the light of the whitish luminary was extinguished by a cavalcade of splintered fracto-cumuli driven by the fury of a low-pressure system centered over Scotland that was showering the earth with sheets of cold rain driven by a howling gale. —*Renaud Fortuner*
Sacramento, Calif.

From time beyond memory, the Indians of the Musoteepak tribe had looked forward each spring to the day when their medicine man, isolated for the winter in his mountain lair, would give them his prediction of things to come by sending a male bovine down the rocky slope wearing either a pale or a dusky blanket, denoting good or evil, and it was with much joy and relief that they heard the lookout perched high in the giant oak respond to their queries by announcing loudly, "Bull wear light one!" —*Charlee Hutton*
Long Beach, Calif.

"That's not Zimbabwe fur," Sheila's voice rang out like a shot, "that's Boer wool, Lytton!" —*Louis Hogan*
Hayward, Calif.

Rebecca sat on the sumptuous chair wearing an equally sumptuous gown watching the brightly costumed dancers swirling to the pulsating music and feeling her cruelly tight shoes press against her oh-so-sensitive pedal digits, when she spied the very courtly portly Lord Bull approach her with outstretched arm for the honor of the next dance and fervently hoped and sincerely prayed that the Bull were light on his feet.
—*Judy Prey*
Sacramento, Calif.

After weighing the ship-bound cargo container to verify that the proper number of crates had been loaded, I darkly stormed over to the hulking night foreman and complained, "Bull, we're light one!"
—*Richard Carter*
Hampton, Va.

"No, lad, he'll never burn that way," the Druid priest said to the novitiate, as he watched the young boy poke the dead white steer with the sacred fire stick, "but if the bull were lit on the end . . ."
—*Wayne D. Worthey*
Washington, D.C.

LYTTONY VI

> **Writing Tip #19: Authenticity** Suppose you want to write a crime story with a police detective for a hero. How do you get insider information on police procedures? Easy, from movies and television, the only reliable sources that your readers will accept as reality.

Famed zoologist Merkin "Scat" Bezoar, who won the National Geographic's prestigious M. Joseph Young Trophy for his exhaustive research concerning the sleeping habits of the Dweebus Futons, rare members of the lowland gorilla family, collected his first scientific sample at the age of three and a half (thin strips of red on his left cheek, which he scrubbed mournfully with a dimpled fist), and made his first cogent theoretical explanation of natural phenomena at the same time, "Cats have needles in their feets."

Kristen Kingsbury Henshaw
Wakefield, Mass.

Jennifer's eyes followed the flickering light as it plummeted to the horizon and exploded in a puffball of flame over the airfield, vaporizing with it the love for Frank which she had cultivated like a Shiitake mushroom in the closet in her apartment, kept under plastic to retain moisture and sprayed with a mixture of distilled water and specially formulated nutrients twice daily until the mushrooms were mature enough to break off the wooden post and saute in olive oil for Frank, who was now probably flambé himself, the poor wretch.

—*Larry Sherman*
Fremont, Calif.

The large, balding man in the rumpled, brown, double-breasted suit balanced his cigar on the glass ashtray as he and Norman reviewed, once again, the plans to make the Bates Motel "The" tourist attraction of this dusty central valley town, thus providing the motel's proprietor with the funds he sought to expand his taxidermy hobby from rabbits, hamsters, and an occasional owl, to larger, more challenging subjects.

—*Don Roberts*
Orinda, Calif.

Gerald smiled cheshirely as the black-and-white pulled around his racy new sports car and drove off into the distance, and silently congratulated himself for coming up with the idea of keeping an emergency box of Winchell's donuts on the back seat, which had once again saved him from yet another speeding ticket. —*Shannon Walker*
Redwood City, Calif.

It began on the frozen banks of the Ob when Dimitri and Anna met in an embrace that turned the normally phlegmatic Siberian into a man possessed with possessing his tiny Steppe sister, a possession that started as he tore off her cape, brutally rent her sable stole, ran his right hand down the front of her Republic cloth coat, scattering buttons over the crystalline carpet, unraveled each of her three sweaters to reveal the one layer of clothing that separated her taut, tawny skin from his trembling fingers—but exhaustion overcame him and, try as he might, Dimitri could not rip Anna's bodice.

—*Len Elliott*
Auburn, Wash.

Cudgel wiped his bloody hand clean on the matted black hairs of his muscular chest and, as his gnarled fingers fumbled with the fragile bra clasp of the pale, lovely, and trembling young woman who was now his captive, he dimly regretted not paying more attention to the foundation-garment ads in his mother's copies of *Good Housekeeping.*   —*T. M. Jacobs*
Minden, Nev.

Creamy, cherry-tipped mounds swaying, heaving, and finally flattening against the upholstery of the back seat, Monique breathlessly vowed never again to serve sundaes on a jeep trip.   —*Timothy Botsko*
San Diego, Calif.

Bethany's glorious breasts glared blatantly from the scandalously low decolletage of her pink ball gown, a pair of succulent water balloons dropped by the Divine Shriner upon unsuspecting males.   —*Cora Williams Weisenberger*
Richton Park, Ill.

Doug was a C programmer—and a damn good one at that—but he was also a big-breast fetishist ("You can never have enough mammary," he often joked in a mass-storage vein . . . " 'mass storage'—sounds like a monstrance, where they kept the host system"); and it was that very oblong obsession that

caused him to refer to the San Jose area, in which he lived and worked, as "Silicone Valley."   —*John A. Barry*
                                            Redwood City, Calif.

Naomi had fallen asleep while sunbathing in the buff, her ample bosom rising and falling with each steady breath like a Bactrian camel at a labored lope.   —*Joyce Hartman*
                                            Plano, Tex.

A Saturday afternoon in November was approaching the time of twilight, which as we all know is the time that the dead rise from the grave to feast on flesh and month-old Miracle Whip.   —*Richard Garrett*
                                            Pittsburgh, Pa.

Clint sat on his horse looking down at the burned-out wagons and the bodies of the massacred family and knew this was no cigar-store Indian he was tracking, when he noticed, high among the rocks to his left, a lone Apache brave regarding him with a wooden expression.   —*Larry Orcutt*
                                            Reseda, Calif.

As he finished off the last of his bourbon, Sidney realized that he was in for another evening of dancing rodents and flying elephants; God, how he hated working the night shift at Disney Studios.   —*James Dainis*
                                            Manhasset, N.Y.

Adam woke with a stitch in his side and a strange woman in his bed.   —*Stephen P. Scheinberg*
                                            Wilmington, Del.

ENTER THE BULWER-LYTTON FICTION CONTEST

The Bulwer-Lytton Fiction Contest is an annual
event that asks entrants to compose the worst possible opening sentence to a novel. Anyone may enter.
The rules are childishly simple:

1) Sentences may be of any length and entrants
   may submit more than one, but all entries must
   be original and previously unpublished.
2) Entries will be judged by category, from "general" to detective, western, science fiction, romance, and so on.
3) Entries should be submitted on index cards, the
   sentence on one side and the entrant's name, address, and phone number on the other.
4) The deadline is April 15 (chosen because Ameri-
   cans associate it with another painful
   submission).

Send your entries to:

> Bulwer-Lytton Fiction Contest
> Department of English
> San Jose State University
> San Jose, CA 95192-0090

FOR THE BEST IN PAPERBACKS, LOOK FOR THE

In every corner of the world, on every subject under the sun, Penguin represents quality and variety—the very best in publishing today.

For complete information about books available from Penguin— including Pelicans, Puffins, Peregrines, and Penguin Classics—and how to order them, write to us at the appropriate address below. Please note that for copyright reasons the selection of books varies from country to country.

In the United Kingdom: For a complete list of books available from Penguin in the U.K., please write to *Dept E.P., Penguin Books Ltd, Harmondsworth, Middlesex, UB7 0DA.*

In the United States: For a complete list of books available from Penguin in the U.S., please write to *Dept BA, Penguin*, Box 120, Bergenfield, New Jersey 07621-0120.

In Canada: For a complete list of books available from Penguin in Canada, please write to *Penguin Books Canada Ltd, 10 Alcorn Avenue, Suite 300, Toronto, Ontario, Canada M4V 3B2.*

In Australia: For a complete list of books available from Penguin in Australia, please write to the *Marketing Department, Penguin Books Ltd, P.O. Box 257, Ringwood, Victoria 3134.*

In New Zealand: For a complete list of books available from Penguin in New Zealand, please write to the *Marketing Department, Penguin Books (NZ) Ltd, Private Bag, Takapuna, Auckland 9.*

In India: For a complete list of books available from Penguin, please write to *Penguin Overseas Ltd, 706 Eros Apartments, 56 Nehru Place, New Delhi, 110019.*

In Holland: For a complete list of books available from Penguin in Holland, please write to *Penguin Books Nederland B.V., Postbus 195, NL-1380AD Weesp, Netherlands.*

In Germany: For a complete list of books available from Penguin, please write to *Penguin Books Ltd, Friedrichstrasse 10-12, D-6000 Frankfurt Main 1, Federal Republic of Germany.*

In Spain: For a complete list of books available from Penguin in Spain, please write to *Longman, Penguin España, Calle San Nicolas 15, E-28013 Madrid, Spain.*

In Japan: For a complete list of books available from Penguin in Japan, please write to *Longman Penguin Japan Co Ltd, Yamaguchi Building, 2-12-9 Kanda Jimbocho, Chiyoda-Ku, Tokyo 101, Japan.*